The Public Sector Leader's Playbook: Avoiding Missteps in an Unforgiving Arena

Trudy Sopp Ph.D.

Praise for *The Public Sector Leader's Playbook: Avoiding Missteps in an Unforgiving Arena*

"Given all the disruptions and complexities in our governance system, effective local government has never been more important. Leading these organizations is extraordinarily challenging. For the leaders, a single misstep can derail vital programs and end promising careers. Trudy outlines the major pitfalls for leaders in the public arena. Leaders today need self-awareness but more importantly, to surround themselves with "truth tellers" to compensate for the blind spots we all have. This is an important companion book to any leadership discussion with topics we too often shy away from."

-Robert J. O'Neill, Jr., Executive in Residence, Joseph P Riley Center for Livable Communities, College of Charleston; former Executive Director, International City/County Management Association (ICMA)

"Public sector leadership is a noble, even sacred profession. Executive behavior and decision-making can enhance or erode public trust, often with long-term emotional and financial consequences. Drawing upon decades of coaching public sector leaders, Dr. Sopp expertly combines on-the-ground experience and leadership theory to provide a roadmap to the self-awareness and contextual knowledge required of leaders to successfully manage themselves and their organizations. My own thirty-year career as a public sector executive would have been enhanced with this kind of insight and advice…this book fills a real gap and need."

-Daryl R. Grigsby, former Public Works Director for the Cities of San Luis Obispo, Pomona, and Kirkland; former Director of Wastewater Treatment in King County; former Director of Transportation, City of Seattle; former Deputy Director, City of San Diego Water and Wastewater System Maintenance Division.

"Dr. Sopp has distilled her life's work into a potent prescription for all current and future leaders in government and higher education. In fact, this masterpiece provides vital insight for leaders in any industry facing media scrutiny, political and constituent pressure, and all the complexities of the 21st century."

-Richel Thaler, former Associate Vice President, San Diego State University

"One after another highly regarded leaders in the public sector...ones seemingly at the top of their game...crashed and burned. Publicly, scandalously, their reputations savaged by the news media. Why did they fail? An even more baffling question: why did these top-level professionals not see it coming? Dr. Sopp's extensive front-line experience shows how to identify warning signs and guard against these calamitous failures. Read this book...before it is too late."

-Randall Christison, former Counsel to the Attorney General of California

"In my consulting in local government and my teaching in social work administration, I found that administrators often had difficulty taking time for important reflection about how they are approaching their work life. This book is packed with valuable and hard-earned practice wisdom, supported by useful conceptual frameworks and an important emphasis on ethics and values. It can be valuable to students and those new to public administration as well as to experienced administrators wanting to engage in self-reflection about...their work in complex organizations and equally complex environments."

-Tom Packard, DSW; Professor Emeritus, School of Social Work, San Diego State University

Trudy Sopp has dedicated her life's work to the pursuit of excellence in public sector leadership. Her ability to articulate hard truths with clarity, courage, and compassion is unparalleled. She challenges leaders to be self-aware, reflect and grow. In this book, she distills years of experience into practical guidance for leaders at all levels.

-Danell Scarborough, Ed.D.; former Executive Director for the City of San Diego Human Relations Commission and Commission on Police Practices; former Director of Administration, San Diego City Attorney's Office; former Adjunct Professor, University of San Diego, Department of Leadership Studies

"The Public Sector Leader's Playbook is an invaluable resource for leaders navigating the complex systems of healthcare and higher education—environments that mirror the dynamics of public sector leadership. Dr. Sopp translates decades of systems scholarship and leadership coaching into a practical guide for recognizing early warning signs, managing personal and organizational risk, and leading with integrity amid political and cultural complexity.

Her framework for understanding system dynamics, leadership liabilities, and mitigative actions resonates deeply with those of us who have led and coached in large, mission-driven organizations. It offers both seasoned and emerging leaders a way to see their context more clearly, anticipate pitfalls, and act with greater awareness and discipline. This is a work of both scholarship and service—an essential playbook for anyone leading in the intricate, high-stakes worlds of government, healthcare, or education."

- Leslie Solomon, Ph.D., Principal, FMG Leading; Lecturer, Fowler College of Business, San Diego State University

Table of Contents

Preface

There is nothing in this book that I haven't said to colleagues, clients, or university students hundreds and hundreds of times. Yet, after four decades in my field, I find it necessary to codify in writing my concerns, advice, and warnings as the patterns I see continue to repeat themselves far too often. Writing this book is something I feel compelled to do. To not do so would contradict everything I believe in as a practitioner in the field of leadership and organization development.

Anyone who has been on the receiving end of my coaching and consulting work or participated in the various leadership programs or college ethics classes I have conducted or overseen has heard me advocate for the imperative of managing one's career in a conscious and effective manner and to do so right through to the end. Over the years, I have witnessed too many dedicated top-level public sector leaders end their careers badly and unnecessarily so. Not only do they suffer losses to their reputations and legacies, but their actions result in damaging consequences to the very organizations or departments they proudly led. This pattern must change.

To mitigate such risks, today's public sector leaders must be dedicated to being uncommonly self-disciplined. The profession now operates in an environment of such staggering complexity that it requires public sector leaders to be especially cognizant of their political environments and highly skilled at navigating them. Leaders must be alert when others rest, and they must listen even when critique is most unwelcome. Today's top-level public sector leaders must be sociologically aware of the roles, relationships, and institutional arrangements that require their deep understanding and attention. Additionally, public sector leaders must be astutely self-aware of the impact of their strengths, deficits, and idiosyncrasies.

How we conduct ourselves and end our careers thus has a significant impact—nothing less than the public good is at stake. The current public sector profession requires this level of consideration, as the current public arena can be unforgiving.

May this book serve as a valuable resource for your team, your students, and yourself.

Trudy Sopp, Ph.D.

San Diego, California

Introduction

The public sector is the arena in which I have spent my entire professional life. I have a finely honed admiration and respect for city managers, city administrators, county chief administrators, special district general managers, and top-level public sector leaders. My admiration for these dedicated professionals comes from observing them up close. Their work occupies center stage, and all eyes are on them. The demands they face cannot be overstated, and the challenges they deal with are so multifaceted as to almost defy description. They hold significant sway over their organizations, regardless of the organization's size. It has been a privilege to work with them and, under their leadership, watch the public service ethic in action. I understand clearly how much harder the role of being a top-level public sector leader is than mine, and I write this book with the hope that the insights offered will aid in furthering this important role and necessary work.

Within the pages of this book, tough feedback, observations, and suggestions are meant to advance the cause and serve the tremendous public ethic we share. I offer these insights from the standpoint of the maxim that if you underestimate or misunderstand the nature of the problem in front of you, you will surely underestimate or misunderstand what is necessary to solve the problem.

I hope we can agree that the public sector is a place where we have to listen closely to both what is said and what remains unsaid, watch with a broad peripheral vision, and solve problems in a way where they don't repeat themselves because *the stakes are simply too high*. It is in this spirit that I invite you to read this book and seriously contemplate the implications it has for your conduct and leadership in the public sector.

Discussing the Undiscussable[1]

I have seen too many public sector leaders forced to end their careers prematurely or badly. Some of these leaders I have consulted with, and others I have watched from afar. These abrupt dissolutions to distinguished careers were painful events to witness. And in my experience, the missteps that led to them are *undiscussable* among many public sector leaders.

It is as though their very discussion suggests blame or fault in the public sector leader, which then feeds the cycle of blame that so dominates public discourse. The elephant in the room is that the patterns underlying these missteps need to be identified, discussed, and analyzed so that they can be solved. We have to discuss the variables involved in these missteps to overcome them or at least manage them better. These missteps have too many consequential impacts to keep them as undiscussable.

About 17 years ago, I began to keep track of public sector leaders in the state of California who had fallen from grace due to a serious "misstep," "misjudgment," or "scandal"[2]. These leaders/managers of public organizations were getting into these situations often, but not always, at the end of their careers. These leaders with excellent reputations, who still had much more to give, were forced to leave overnight because of these missteps.

An astute colleague, Craig Dunn, Ph.D., and I often discussed the source of this constant stream of fallen heroes and heroines. Dr. Dunn frequently presented on ethical decision-making during management academies I facilitated. Schooled in philosophy and business, he characterized these missteps as "ethical lapses"[3]. However, as a sociologist, I countered that this conclusion was too psychological and individualistic. There is a social pattern here, I argued. These events occurred too frequently and across too many different organizations. I suspected that there was something external—structural—that was driving this. These people were too good at their jobs, too dedicated, and too professional, and they had spent years devoted to the public interest. Dr. Dunn encouraged me to identify and articulate the patterns I was seeing.[4]

I began to focus on the serious impact that these missteps had on the leader's team and organization. When an established leader is abruptly ushered out, and a new leader is brought in, a team or

4

organization has no choice but to deal with many unanticipated consequences. I noted that many of the new leaders were often simply not ready for the job or not accepted because they had not won the hearts and minds of the staff. In these instances, the power dynamics shift from a typical, reasonable, and established balance to that of confusion and dysfunction. Individual team members vying for their organizational interests and needs, and a new "in-group" made possible only by the power vacuum left by the former leader, would compete against the new leader for influence. Team morale and productivity would go down, and time and money spent recovering from staff turnover would run up the balance books. In Chapter One, a case study is used to demonstrate the typical impact of a serious misstep or "scandal" on a public organization. From the realignment of the power dynamics internally and externally to the inevitable plummeting employee morale to the citizen backlash due to a lack of confidence in the offending public organization.

Although fallen leaders may reboot their careers with another organization, they inevitably take with them hurtful, unspoken, and lingering questions that affect others' perceptions of them. I tracked these dynamic movements because I have a stake in the successful functioning of this profession, as I have made a decades-long career out of worrying about the profession of public administration as an entity. Furthermore, as a sociologist, I observed a pattern in these departures.

In studying these missteps more closely, I tested my assumptions and thinking and wrestled with whether the "trouble" was linked simply to staying too long in a position. Then, I studied my assumptions some more. I am now ready to share my thoughts, hence this book. The breadth and depth of the experiences, observations, and analyses presented here were drawn from throughout the state of California, and given the complexity that exists, I believe they have implications for every town, city, and county in the country.

The patterns I observed and documented established that these series of missteps were about much more than individual "ethical lapses." The multifaceted environmental factors that affect all aspects of the functioning of public organizations today are stunningly complicated and rapidly changing. Thus, explaining the patterns in public sector leadership missteps or scandals in terms of ethical lapses is almost quaint and perhaps naïve, given the dynamic environment in which public leaders operate. This explains why established required ethics training does little to mitigate the trouble leaders get into – the trouble is far more layered than knowledge of the legal guidelines and parameters can address.

First, it is an indisputable fact that the environments that top-level public sector leaders work in nowadays are so dynamic, so political, so culturally and technologically transformative, and so under the microscope of the public, the press, and regulatory agencies that unanticipated trouble seems almost inevitable. These issues arise when they are least expected, when there are no perceived warning signs or when the signs are simply overlooked. Leading in the public sector during times of societal, organizational, and uncertain political dynamics has always been challenging, given budget constraints and structural budget deficits. Thus, to lead in today's environment is to deal with previously unimagined challenges and demands. Past assumptions and practices will become obsolete, and leaders who fail to learn and adapt are doomed to learn the hard way and, in the process, damage what has otherwise been an exemplary career and hurt the organizations they came to serve. Chapter Two provides detailed diagrams and descriptions of the enormous contextual and structural variables that face public sector top-level leaders.

The complexity does not end here; a leader's history within their organization can become a factor, too. Over the course of a long and distinguished career in the public sector, a minor incident and a lingering conflict are not out of the ordinary. A bridge or two may even have been burned. However, these slights might come back to bite leaders in the form of a public disclosure of a moment of exaggeration or a questionable judgment they made. Some elected officials or other municipal agency members could be lying in the cool grass, waiting to make the most of an opportunity to pile on a mistake.

Without having to think deeply, I could list one mid-level manager and three top-level leaders from the same city whose names appeared in the local newspaper and online media platforms within the same week. These media outlets are often looking for any story that might sell a newspaper or increase online readership. Each of these leaders was involved in a complex negotiation with a public agency or a private sector business, and all were trying to figure out how to create a win-win situation and propose solutions that benefited all parties, including their organizations. In each case, there was a player or interest group who found the negotiation worthy of a public challenge or questioned the stakeholders involved—that is, the public opinion was that the deal-making process and actions were unacceptable at best and unethical or illegal at worst. Maybe the details disclosed were true, and maybe they weren't. However, the truth often doesn't matter once sensational information is co-opted by the media/public arena. The well-crafted reputations that each of these prior leaders had worked 10, 25, or 30 years to create were tarnished in a matter of minutes. The unspoken perception of the public was, "If they didn't do anything wrong, why were their names in the news?".

My answer is that the current public sector reality requires a level of self-discipline and self-awareness when we least expect to require it. In Chapters Three and Four, I discuss in detail the personal factors like beliefs, mental models, and leadership skills that leaders bring to the mix and their potential ethical blind spots as they navigate the complex current context and current structural arrangements. I realize that this undiscussable, on top of all the other environmental variables that require juggling, can feel overwhelming to handle, like an uninvited guest who gives you feedback you didn't ask for or criticism you didn't invite. I ask this of the profession, of you, the future of public sector leadership, to open the door to this discussion.

The resistance I experience when I present on this topic or when I coach or offer advice to a leader who is on the precipice of a misstep is often dismaying and potentially irresponsible on their part, given that they occupy such important leadership roles. The resistance to the discussion, the rationalizations, and the unspoken belief that there is a criticism just below the surface invariably lead to negative reactions from the top-level public sector leader, with them saying, "Don't worry, I heard you", or changing the subject entirely.

Here, I remind you why you are in this business in the first place: to serve the public. The public is not well-served by these painful departures and their disruptive consequences. This is a reality that the public sector profession needs to recognize and address. In Chapter Five, I identify the red flags that should be noticed, that speak loudly within the organization, that trouble is ahead, and that need to be acted upon by the top-level leader to avoid more serious missteps, misjudgments, or scandals. Chapter Six identifies what steps the leader should consider to mitigate a glaring misstep and preventive actions to take to recover from or gracefully exit a scandal.

Over Four Decades in the Public Sector

For more than four decades, I have provided management consulting services to promote the effectiveness of public organizations. Working with top-level public sector leaders, managers, and supervisors in governmental and public agencies, I have tackled issues involving leadership/management development and performance, productivity improvement, process and system improvement, citizen satisfaction with services, employee job satisfaction at all levels, and creating a more inclusive and respectful workplace. This section references the professional experience that informs the observations and insights presented in this book.

As the Manager of the City of San Diego's Organization Effectiveness Program (OEP), a public sector unit that consisted of 22 internal analysts and organization development (OD) specialists, I oversaw the task of facilitating and guiding change in an organization which employed 10,000 employees. The OEP's purpose was to utilize analytic and organization development skills and techniques to improve productivity, increase employee job satisfaction, and enhance citizen satisfaction with city services. With significant departmental data and analysis in hand, the OEP facilitated problem-solving and action-planning workshops across the organization. Many of the workshops involved team building, conflict resolution and skill training, and coaching of supervision staff. Management and supervisory academies and timely professional development topics were offered organization-wide.

My OEP role included managing the teams and interventions and liaising with the city manager, their executive team, and departmental directors about implementation issues. This required navigating the power dynamics of making changes in a large organization, influencing the top leader's commitment and action toward making the organization more effective, and becoming a trusted partner in the improvement process.

Additionally, in the early 90s, the City of San Diego organization faced the growing need to create a more inclusive and respectful work environment. The City's leadership, through the work of the OEP team, created a Diversity Commitment effort. With guidance provided by the Kaleel Jamison Consulting Group, a four-day diversity academy was implemented throughout the organization. These four-day sessions and the numerous problem-solving task forces and working groups that evolved out of them began to change, for the better, the culture, behaviors, and treatment of an entire 10,000-person workforce. The lessons learned about respectful treatment were numerous and stay with me today. It was the most complex, multifaceted, bold and values-driven effort this organization had ever undertaken.

The work of the OEP team led to a national reputation for conducting educational sessions on diversity. Throughout the region numerous organizations were asking the OEP team for help, as they did not have the internal resources or expertise to provide OD programs or diversity educational academies. In 1993, upon approval by the San Diego City Council and under the management of the city manager, I proposed a public sector leadership institute for the San Diego region called THE CENTRE for Organization Effectiveness. THE CENTRE was an enterprise fund extension of the internal OEP organization and would serve as a one-stop shop for public agencies in the region.[5]The core CENTRE team and a pool of skilled OD consultants offered services to develop leaders and managers, conducted OD interventions, offered professional development trainings and survey self-assessment instruments, and provided private coaching sessions, diversity educational academies, and facilitation skills as needed.

THE CENTRE eventually grew into a statewide public sector entity, a California Joint Powers Authority (JPA).[6] As the founding executive director of THE CENTRE, my experience and reach ultimately expanded across the state. Those who have sought me out through THE CENTRE for executive coaching, management consulting, OD expertise, training and professional development, organizational assessment, and city council, board, or general workshop facilitation include: city managers; county executives and administrators; general managers of large, medium, and small-sized water agencies; city/county department directors; large-scale health care institution executives; university administrators; public agency and non-profit directors; elected officials, such as mayors, city council members, state legislators, and water board members; various city/county/state boards, and commissions; and several thousand mid-level public sector managers across the state of California who attended THE CENTRE leadership academies.[7]

Tracking Missteps: Data and Approach

About 17 years ago, I began to engage with clients and colleagues on the concept of missteps. I went about this by bringing up my concerns, coaching clients who were facing the ramifications of poor judgments, weaving the subject into the leadership presentations and university ethics classes I taught, and writing about how many careers were ending badly for public sector leaders and managers. When I began to notice a pattern in these departures, I observed, noted, and kept records of public communications about these missteps, how they were characterized by the media, and how they were documented in newspaper articles and online media coverage. If I knew the stakeholders involved, I made a note of my knowledge of the parties, the variables involved, the types of actions and behaviors taken, and their organizations' reactions. I compared my notes to the theories and patterns I had already identified on ethics in my writings and presentations on the subject.

Refining my thinking continuously, I kept track of the types of behaviors and circumstances referenced and the patterns in them and did so in a replicable and systematic manner. Many of these leaders I knew through my work in the public sector, and just as many were strangers. I then reflected on these behaviors retrospectively, not at the time a particular leader consulted me. To warn future business leaders of these pitfalls, I used publicized examples in the ethics classes I taught at the Fowler College of Business. Similarly, these examples were used in CENTRE leadership academy presentations on how to face ethical dilemmas and resolve ethical issues in the public sector. Thus, there were many opportunities for reactions, revisions, and objections from public sector practitioners about the conclusions I was drawing. None came.

Over time, and when the occasion allowed, I checked in with as many of these leaders as possible in later interviews or discussions as they and their colleagues reflected on the incidents or missteps. These behaviors, the circumstances, and the contexts in which these leaders operated were grouped as common data through a content analysis process.

Specifically, the analysis of these data led me to propose a set of theoretical concepts about public sector environments, identify common blind spots among public sector leaders, formulate advice on red flags, and cull what has worked in my years of experience giving such advice. Thus, I am confident in offering fix-its or actions that can be taken to mitigate or resolve a misstep. Additionally, I tested my thinking in my daily consulting work and, specifically, with a keynote presentation to an audience of over 1,500 city managers and top-level public sector leaders at a League of California Cities City Managers Annual Conference that took place in February 2020 in Napa, California.

My work has also been influenced by a set of ethical framework concepts from the ethics literature and my sociological training. In this book, you will find an original conceptual framework I developed for contextual and structural variables (Chapter Two, "Staggering Complexity: The Contextual Variables that Impact Public Sector Management Careers") found in typical public sector organizations that impact behavior and decision-making.

Additionally, I have observed, identified, and analyzed a set of personal beliefs, mindsets, and skills (Chapter Three, "Personal Factors that Impact Judgment and Behavior") that public leaders often bring to the profession and contribute to the complex set of variables that influence their behaviors. This is original thinking and analysis based on observations gathered over time and framed by a grounded theory approach. Ethical blind spots[8] are identified and explained in Chapter Four, "Blind Spots that Lead to Errors in Judgment." Furthermore, they are categorized during the analysis of the data and scenarios referenced in the book.

The major variables in Chapters Two and Three have changed only slightly since my initial conversations with Dr. Dunn during our collaboration in 2007 (referenced in the "Introduction" Chapter). It is important to note how consistent and reliable the variables identified in the diagrams and chapters on context, structural arrangements, and the personal factors leaders bring and face have been over time. Even as administrations change and new federal, state, and local leaders take office, the contexts and structures public leaders face and the beliefs, mindsets, skills, and blind spots (Chapter Four) they bring have a consistency to them that allowed me to draw my conclusions and make the suggestions offered in Chapters Five ("Red Flags: Signals of Trouble Ahead) and Six ("Antidotes and Mitigative Actions"). The field of ethical decision-making research in the workplace[9] heavily influenced my thinking on blind spots.

On Confidentiality and Ethics

Nearly all of the (perceived) problematic behaviors detailed in this book were reported by public media, so they were not confidential missteps, misjudgments, or scandals. Even so, I have thought long and hard about how to convey the missteps and the lessons to be learned from them without the reader becoming intrigued by the identities of the stakeholders or agencies involved and wanting to focus on that part of the story. Ultimately, I decided that the most powerful way for me to convey these important lessons is to use real-life examples so that the reader understands their serious repercussions on organizations and careers. In the current environment, it is easy for public, real-life examples to devolve into a "tell-all." My concerns about the ethics of this dilemma have delayed the completion of this book by months and months, as I have wrestled with what is the right thing to do and how best to achieve my purposes. Consequently, I chose to adopt the following strategy:

1) For a majority of the real-life examples, I cite public information (i.e., information published in the media) about individuals and agencies. These media references and resources are listed chronologically in Appendix B: "Chronological List of Select Reference Materials and Articles on Missteps, Misjudgments, and Scandals" and not in the body of the manuscript or in the endnotes. Should the reader wish, they can read these references and review them independently of this book. In this way, the focus of the book stays on the analysis provided and the lessons intended and not on an individual or agency.

2) In the few cases where I use an example that was not covered in the media, where the source of the action remains confidential and was not public, additional information can be found in the "Endnotes" section with the reference: "Citation source confidential." I have only ever used this approach to make a point about a serious lesson to be learned. Usually, this issue has tripped up far too many public sector leaders and is a repeated pattern I have witnessed. While the media has not written about it, I feel the behavior, action, or blind spot must be disclosed, given the purpose of this book.

3) Even with the above steps, to ensure identities remain protected and to allow the reader to track an example or individual's actions throughout the book when I refer to them more than

once, I will be using pseudonyms like "Mr. Charisma," and "Ms. Big Picture Thinker." In all other cases, I will use the term "big city top-level public sector leader" or "small county top-level public sector leader" or neutral agency descriptions like "Regional Transportation Agency," "Municipal Water Agency," "big city," and "medium-sized city" etc.

4) Because public sector organizations and positions across the country use different titles at the highest two or three levels (e.g., city manager, city administrator, town administrator, county administrative officer, county executive officer, general manager of a water district/agency, general manager of a special district, chief operating officer, department director, deputy director, and deputy chief operating officer), I have elected to use the term "top-level public sector leader" to represent them all to ensure the terminology is understandable to the nationwide audience of this book.

5) To test my conclusions, which are presented in Chapter Six, "Antidotes and Mitigative Actions," regarding actions to take to recover from missteps, I interviewed several retired top-level public sector leaders to learn how they stayed out of trouble throughout the course of their careers. Many of their insights I had already identified myself in the course of my data collection and analysis. This fact increased the face validity of the advice they provided. To give credit where it is due, I acknowledge these interviewees in my "Acknowledgements" section. Those interviewees referenced by a pseudonym in the book gave explicit permission for the quote(s). Any interviewees or public sector leaders quoted were asked to review parts or all of this book to ensure that their thoughts were properly interpreted and characterized.

Word of Caution

Perhaps as you read this book, you will have some of the following thoughts:

- This won't happen to me.

- I am different.

- I am smarter than others.

- I am better at politics than others.

- By bringing this up, are you suggesting I did something wrong?

- This feels like an exaggeration. Are you suggesting that we should not take risks?

These responses are completely understandable. However, for the top-level public leaders, they are not. To serve the public good and the public's need for effective local government services, leaders must: be thorough when they least feel like it, be reflective when they are most fatigued; maintain their focus on the biggest picture possible; and anticipate the consequences and unintended consequences of their actions.

We must stop considering missteps in isolation or attributing them to certain regions, cities, or counties that are particularly difficult to manage or especially political environments. They happen in both big and small places, and just like the system archetype of the slowly eroding or "drifting" goals concept or the "slippery slope,"[10] they chip away at the reputation and nobility of the public sector.

Often, the person who calls out inappropriate behaviors or highlights possible missteps is labeled by the leader or their colleagues as a "naysayer" or a "Suzie Doomsday." Take, for example, the well-known O-ring engineers on the NASA Challenger Shuttle team. They were labeled by management as caring only about the O-rings when they persisted in sharing the dire message not to launch; the lead engineer was criticized for not having on his "management hat" or adopting the executive perspective, and the pressure caused them to recant and give in to the pressure to launch.[11]

I, myself, have felt relationships go south when I have given tough feedback to leaders that their actions or blind spots might get them in trouble. I have presented this very warning to conference audiences and felt the room grow intensely interested yet oddly quiet at the prospect. Even when unsure about whether readers might receive my stance with open-minded questions, I must persist. This book is a product of my persistence. It is offered to you with both an unwavering respect for the profession and a stark warning.

Endnotes

[1] The concept of "undiscussables" in organizations was originally explored by C. Argyris (1990) in *Overcoming Organizational Defenses* and brought to life by W. R. Noonan (2007) in *Discussing the Undiscussable: A Guide to Overcoming Defensive Routines in the Workplace*. My use of the term here reflects the group dynamic on teams and in organizations, where the real problem, or "elephant" in the room, is not discussed because discussing it would be undiscussable. Often, the undiscussable is the leader and the leader's behavior or admitting to the leader and/or an elected body that a capital project they approved moved forward on faulty assumptions discovered by staff after the fact. I consider the topic of this book to be an undiscussable because, especially in the public sector, any mistake or misstep is under such scrutiny that it can end a career and/or undermine faith in government institutions. Admitting that these missteps happen in the public sector is an undiscussable. However, if we don't discuss this and problem-solve as to how to avoid these missteps, the vicious cycle repeats itself.

[2] It is important to clarify that I am including the term "scandal" here because it is the term used by electronic and print media as well as social media. I do not consider a misstep or misjudgment the same as a scandal, although either could evolve into a scandal depending on the follow-up actions taken. All three terms are used throughout this manuscript.

[3] I had this discussion with Craig Dunn, Ph.D., in 2007 while planning an ethical decision-making presentation and potential ethics article.

[4] As I identified these more sociological and public sector-specific patterns, Dr. Dunn was particularly helpful in encouraging me to articulate the "mindsets" variables. At the time of our collaboration, Dr. Dunn was an Associate Professor Emeritus at San Diego State University and a senior CENTRE consultant. He recently retired as a Wilder

Distinguished Professor of Business and Sustainability (2016–2023) at Western Washington University, where he was also Dean of the College of Business and Economics (2013–2016).

[5] The City of San Diego City Council approved the creation of THE CENTRE for Organization Effectiveness as an enterprise fund department on November 9, 1993. See San Diego City Council docket resolution #282972. Enterprise fund departments charge a fee for their services.

[6] As THE CENTRE grew in scope and size, the San Diego City Attorney's Office, the City Auditor, and the Personnel Department felt it was prudent to spin THE CENTRE out as its own entity. After much research by THE CENTRE's attorney, a JPA structure was proposed. This structure requires two governmental entities to agree to create a third entity. The San Diego County Water Authority (SDCWA) agreed to join the City of San Diego in the creation of THE CENTRE for Organization Effectiveness. The City of San Diego City Council approved the creation of THE CENTRE for Organization Effectiveness on September 12, 2000; resolution #293816. The SDCWA approved the creation of the JPA known as THE CENTRE for Organization Effectiveness on September 28, 2000.

[7]After passing the baton in 2007, I moved into the Centre's consultant pool as an independent contractor under the banner Sopp Consulting, Inc., and continued to work with public organizations until my semi-retirement in the fall of 2021. A partial listing of clients I worked with over the course of my career is detailed in Appendix A. I continue to engage in periodic coaching and consulting, workshop facilitation for select elected officials, and presentations as they relate to my research and writing.

In 2010, new CENTRE leadership revised the name to lower case, "The Centre for Organization Effectiveness." Both the logo and color scheme were updated. The Centre continues to serve the region, the state of California, and beyond with a talented and dedicated staff and pool of savvy consultants. For more information, contact the current Centre CEO, Sommer Kehrli, Ph.D., at www.tcfoe.com

[8] A "blind spot" is a term that refers to aspects of our behavior that we may not be able to see that, among other impacts, often have ethical consequences for ourselves and others. My use of the term in my analysis and my categorization of behaviors was heavily influenced by the work of Bazerman & Tenbrunsel (2013) in *Blind Spots: Why We Fail to Do What's Right and What to do About It*. I credit them with conceptually capturing important ethical lapses and articulating them clearly and precisely in their work.

[9] Bazerman & Tenbrunsel (2013); Collins (2009); Trevino & Nelson (2017).

[10] A good overview and explanation of systems archetypes can be found in *The Fifth Discipline Field Book Strategies and Tools for Building a Learning Organization,* by Peter Senge et al. (1994), pp. 121–150.

[11] See *Groupthink, Revised Edition* by CRM Films (1998, DVD release). This unique film presents a reenactment and analysis of the phone conferences between the engineers and management that led up to the final, and tragic, decision to launch the 1986 Space Shuttle Challenger.

Chapter One

High Stakes: Why Missteps, Misjudgments, and Scandals Matter So Much

On a too frequent basis, top-level public sector leaders are facing the career and reputational consequences of a misstep, misjudgment, or "scandal" in their organization, irrespective of where their organization resides in the country. Their organizational and political environments are extraordinarily complex. This environment, intertwined with the top-level public sector leader's beliefs, mindsets, skills, and potential blind spots, can create a perfect storm for them and the organization they seek to serve. The following six chapters will underscore this reality, document the impacts and consequences for public sector leaders and their organizations, and identify mechanisms and actions for you, the reader, to contemplate as you reflect on the implications for your public sector career.

The following is an example of a misstep, misjudgment, or, as the label local media likes to say, a "scandal." While the terms are sometimes used interchangeably, I do not consider a misstep or misjudgment the same as a "scandal." However, each could evolve into a scandal depending on the types of actions taken or not taken by the public sector leader or public organization.

Picture in your mind a big-city regional transportation agency (RTA). This organization is admirable. It has a vision and purpose unlike any other in the region. It is the region's major planning entity for transportation planning, housing analysis, transit construction, environmental standards, and public safety demographics and analysis. It has a board that represents the region's cities, county, and major agency stakeholders, and this board votes on policy decisions based on staff analysis and recommendations. This RTA is staffed by demographers, economists, data analysts, planners, transportation experts in policy and construction, and other professionals who are well-educated, thoughtful, creative, and visionary. This organization is respected and appreciated, and their charismatic and articulate leader is adored. Mr. Charisma had a several-decades-long career in the public sector and was exemplary at navigating the public arena.

After a year of questions about the facts surrounding a failed ballot initiative his organization supported and led, and an audit by an external fact-finding firm about the role his staff played in providing the background facts for this measure, he faced an undoubtedly crushing headline. The local newspaper stated he was about to retire amid a "scandal" at the RTA. The consequences for this RTA were numerous and created challenges for its reputation and staff for at least three years, if not longer.

Case Example:

In December 2016, the big city's RTA board voted to approve a 4% increase in pay for the executive director, Mr. Charisma. He had been thinking of retiring, but the board wanted him to stay, so he did. He was at the height of his influence in both his organization and the region, and he had a board chair he was loyal to and who had one remaining year as chair. It can be fairly speculated that he agreed to continue in the position because he wanted his chair's legacy and the region to successfully achieve the important transportation initiatives that were on the table at the time. The staff had done the hard work of preparing a 2016 ballot initiative to increase this RTA's revenue to pave the way for future transportation projects. However, the initiative failed at the ballot box.

It is worth noting that there were some who had encouraged the executive director to retire at the top of his game and influence. Some were convinced that the environment was getting more politicized, polarized, and complex and that tough years were ahead. He did not take this advice.

As is common for any large public project, there were many interest groups and local news reporters who had their eyes trained on the actions of this agency.

Environmental groups and public transit advocates had long complained that Mr. Charisma had been too focused on improving freeways and roads at the expense of transit and bicycle infrastructure. There was growing tension and polarization on his board about this very issue. His supporters, however, praised him as an effective advocate for transportation needs at the state and federal levels and as someone who was effective at securing state and federal funds for important projects.

When the initiative failed, the media devoted much ink to reflecting on this failure. At some point, there was a staff leak to a local news source. This leak suggested that the staff-forecasted economic projections used to justify the initiative had been inaccurate and had under-projected how much the projects would cost to complete and that staff had not been united in how the projections were characterized and presented to the higher ups.

This story prompted the board to order an independent investigation in 2017 into what had become called by one local news outlet "The [Big City RTA's] Revenue Forecasting Scandal." A local public news station summarized the findings of this investigation, claiming the RTA overstated how much money it could collect from the sales tax initiative to pay for the transportation projects and underestimated how much the projects would cost to complete. Investigators found that executives at the agency responded to the scandal poorly, and the lack of transparency about forecasting errors created the appearance of a cover-up.

This scrutiny had numerous consequences: the abrupt retirement of a beloved and valued executive director, a reputation that was tarnished by troubling findings asserting that the culture of the organization might not have encouraged contrary opinions during the decision-making process; the intrusion of the state legislature into the structural make-up and voting process of the RTA board, prompting legislation that consequently divided the board, some would say permanently, around partisan lines; a demoralized and beleaguered staff that found themselves fallen from grace in the eyes of the regional cities, counties, and agencies that depended on this RTA for reliable analysis; and internal recriminations and examinations by staff, supporters, and critics.

A new executive director, Mr. Controversial Visionary, was selected a little over a year later, and a realignment of power, influence, initiatives, vision, and boldness was introduced. The careers of numerous RTA staff ended in the intervening year. Furthermore, questions were raised, with a gnawing persistence, about the *investigation: "What really happened here?" "What isn't being said?" "Who knew what when?" This is a typical reaction when there is a belief that the executive director fell on the sword to end the story or stop the scrutiny of the organization. Or, the belief could have been that investigative reports can only go so far. Once a retirement is announced, the story is generally considered over.*

Your organization and career both matter. Let's look at the negative impacts a misstep, misjudgment, or scandal can have on an organization and a career. This was not a hard section for me to write as I have seen these impacts time and again.

- **The power dynamics are completely upended**; there might be a power void, but more likely, there will be a quick shift in who is in or out. None of this is to the benefit of the goals and projects already in place. For example, `after one top-level public leader's retirement from a regional water agency, which was prompted by health issues and media speculation that a couple of embarrassing missteps had hastened this departure, the board chair announced: "there's a new sheriff in town." This quickly set in motion region-wide questions about what this might mean about the future policy direction of the board or about staffing within the agency. Another top-level public leader of a big city's medium-sized redevelopment agency refused to leave his organization, even after behind-the-scene negotiations between him and a board representative. This back and forth created a quiet power struggle scandal within the organization and a dynamic that angered and empowered the board to insert themselves more into the day-to-day operations. Once the top-level leader finally left, the board became much more directive with the next new leader they hired. This was an abrupt change in the historically and decades-long reasonable power dynamic between the board and its organizational leader. As this day-to-day oversight became untenable to the new leader and suspicions and dissatisfaction over roles erupted, there was turnover in the leadership role once again, turmoil in the board's internal power dynamics, and morale issues among the staff ensued.

- **Rationalizations or actions to cover embarrassment can ensue**, and these behaviors are time-consuming to handle for the leader at the center of the scandal and for managers at all levels. Employee gossip takes up time and keeps the scandals and missteps alive. A 2019 meta-analysis published in the journal *Social Psychological and Personality Science* about workplace gossiping showed that employees spent about 52 minutes a day, on average, gossiping. Another study found that nearly 75% of white-collar workers gossiped, and 30% of employees said that this was their main source of information. These percentages vary based on generational groups. Often, gossiping is not negative, per se, and it serves as a way for employees to make sense of what happened and seek affirmation about the current state of things.[1] This need to re-litigate or discuss events to understand what happened oftentimes goes on for several years if there is no published investigation or public explanation into the sequence of events, who did what, or the consequences for the parties when a particularly egregious misstep has taken place. Seeds of doubt could remain regarding the factors that allowed the misstep to happen in the first place. To this day, the big city's RTA continues to deal with fresh fears from citizens, businesses, and the media that they cannot be trusted. Any new scrutiny of the organization, even five years later, is seen through the lens of the 2017 scandal.

- **The fix is often worse than the problematic event.** Inevitably, a board of supervisors, city council, regulatory agency, higher-level authority, or, sometimes, citizen group steps in to correct the problem—and they make it worse. At least a third of the board members of the big city's RTA would argue that the state legislation that changed the RTA's voting structure, using the scandal as the rationale, made the board's decision-making more problematic and divisive for years to come. The corrective actions taken by a council, a board, a legislative body, or voting citizens are not generally poorly designed on purpose. This is an inevitable system archetype, called "fixes that fail", that occurs when fixes are not well thought out, usually when there is little time to react or when the spun news story has taken over, and quick action is required to save face or manage an organization's image.

For example, a charter change to the strong mayor form of governance was voted in by citizens in one big city soon after the underfunding of this big city employee pension system was made public. This scandal involved no personal financial gain. This underfunding, which had been voted on and approved by the city council, was seen by some leaders in the community as an example of the excess power of the city manager/council form of government. That is, the city manager knew the budget better than the council members and moved money around to free up funds for general projects, including projects requested by the city council, mayor, and citizen initiatives. In the case of the underfunding of the employee pension system, this was done to free up money for general fund use and shore up the city's bond-funding status for various redevelopment projects at a time when the city's investments were doing quite well in the stock market, and the funds were to be paid back once the underfunding hit a certain benchmark. This was an action approved by the city council in plain sight of the public.

A few years later, a decision was made by this big city's top-level public sector leader and his big city council to further underfund the pension system and to go below the benchmark originally designated. This was when the actions caused a reaction. A concerned citizen learned of the underfunding action as a result of her position on the retirement board, and a formal complaint prompted SEC, FBI, and in-house City Attorney's Office investigations. This was considered a huge local scandal.

The point here is not to dissect the scandals but to focus on the impact these scandals and missteps had on the public sector players and their organizations. Subsequently, a big city newspaper editorial, the same editorial that referenced the perceptions about the big city's RTA, made the following point: "More than 15 years after city leaders were revealed to have played fast and loose with city finances to disguise the damage done by decisions to intentionally underfund pensions programs, the city ... is still haunted by a trust gap".[2]

Unproven accusations during the investigations into the pension scandal ended careers prematurely and caused the unceremonious departures of several talented, hard-working, and long-time public servants who incurred extensive financial costs to prove their innocence. The years of long investigations found no legal wrongdoing, but the strong mayor "fix" became the basis for a successful ballot measure led by citizens and civic leaders. This initiative completely changed the structure of the big city's charter and government from a city manager/city council form, where policy decisions are made by the city council and operational implementation is conducted by the city manager and staff, to a strong mayor form of government, where the mayor's office proposes policies and a budget and oversees the operational departments. In a strong mayor form of government, depending on the circumscribed powers outlined in the charter, other departments like the city council, the auditor, the city attorney, and perhaps an independent budget office do not report to the mayor.

This specific misstep and scandal I observed up close is significant to the findings of this book. The patterns of behavior involved, the ethical blind spots, and the contextual decisions made have replicated themselves in numerous other city and county government settings, albeit with varying consequences, but they were no less damaging to the stakeholders involved.

- If the problem leads to a top-level staff departure, **there is a tendency for the replacement to be a "safe" choice or an "opposite style" choice to the previous leader**; somehow, this person contrasts with the previous problematic or risk-taking leader. Often, if at a departmental level, the position is eliminated or reorganized as punishment for the embarrassment.

Furthermore, when the departure of a top-level public sector leader coincides with a scandal before or after they leave, the elected body often concludes that "things need to change around here," and they select a "weaker" leader that they are more likely to control and influence so that what happened before won't happen again.

- **The institution at large loses credibility in the community** and pays the price for years to come when a scandal occurs. Trust is eroded in ways difficult to document, but a lack of trust yields behaviors such as more pushback from citizens at community meetings or more pushback on staff proposals by the boards of these public agencies. This distrust could be even more subtle; it can manifest as phone calls, emails, and other forms of outreach to the offending organization through editorials, letters to the editor, and social media blogs.

Furthermore, the organization's leadership is generally not promptly replaced permanently (many interim appointments) or is not taken as seriously as they were pre-scandal. As in the case of the big city's move to a strong mayor as a "fix" to the pension under-funding scandal, there was a voluntary exodus of a large number of top and mid-level leaders who found the governance concept of a strong mayor untenable. This exodus necessitated the promotion of many staff into positions they were not ready for. There was initially significant confusion and disorganization in the organization's day-to-day decision-making, roles, and responsibilities, and consequently, a noticeable impact on service delivery to citizens.

Information and influence are power in the public arena, and the troubled organization has to work its way back into good graces, just like a poor performer would have to. This can take years. Talk to any RTA staff about this and any public sector employee about the gray cloud of public perceptions that hangs over their pensions.

- **There are reorganizations**, new goals, new players, process improvements, and entirely new financial structures that could occur. Some are needed, and many are not, but they are put in place because a "fix" was called for.

- Lastly, **employee morale plummets** and could stay there for three to five years, if not more, following a scandal. Sometimes, there are changes for the good, and at other times, there are simply changes. We can all generally agree that a scandal is not the best way to make change happen.

What happens here is that employees who excel will only accept being treated badly by citizens and elected officials (who often direct their frustrations toward remaining employees) for so long. They leave and take their experience and talent with them. Those who stay remember the wounds, and this can create risk-averse behaviors, meaning innovation and change take even longer.

To be clear, there have been successful cases of the next phases where a top-level public sector leader sweeps in, reframes the dynamics, takes over, and brings joy once again. I can name the cities and agencies in which these scenarios have occurred. However, these are often hard fought; creating new environments or revamping damaged ones is extremely taxing on the first string of pioneers, and it is often the next generation that reaps the benefits. Ask any leader who came in after a big misstep or scandal. Bouncing back, particularly from a scandal, takes years and years, and the new players who don't even know the history of an organization are usually the ones to benefit most from recovery efforts. Organizations typically change after these scandals, and many of the changes can eventually yield better fiscal policies, additional structural and ethical parameters such as new positions that provide oversight, new reporting relationships, new structures that may provide more equity, and role clarification between boards and their leaders.

A misstep or scandal is not the way to induce these changes, as they rarely lead to the most thoughtful sets of actions. This matters if you are running an organization and prefer not to be reactive but proactive. This also matters if you care about the reputation and effectiveness of the public sector. This especially matters given that a public scandal can create a lack of trust among citizens, and their reluctance to approve new projects or tax measures can delay infrastructure projects. Thus, scandals play a significant role in the future careers of innumerable public sector leaders and the disruptive ripple effects on their teams. The consequential nature of missteps, misjudgments, and scandals requires that we, as public servants, be at our best at all times and do what is necessary to ensure that we stay there.

Chapter Two

Staggering Complexity: The Contextual Variables that Impact Public Management Careers

The context in which top-level public sector leaders operate harbor variables that must be noticed and mastered. Three major variables are: **1)** the environments in which decisions are made, **2)** the uncontrollable complexities they face, and **3)** the hand they have been dealt as a result of the decisions of elected officials and citizens. They influence and often are the containers in which everyone's actions are taken, and careers are impacted. It is this larger context within which public agencies are situated that unambiguously makes the case that missteps cannot be accounted for simply by a personal or individual inadequacy in the players managing complex organizations. While leadership and character flaws may contribute, a large percentage of missteps can be linked to the following tremendously complex, ever-changing, and dynamic contextual and structural variables coalescing at the same time. *Failure on the part of the leader to see this is the highly consequential misstep.*

In 2013, Bob O'Neill, then executive director of the International City/County Management Association (ICMA), published a seminal article, "Leadership and the Profession: Where to From Here?".[3] Drawing on input from ICMA members, relevant stakeholders, and subsequent further research, the article identified five key drivers of local government for the next decade (which they acknowledged could vary by complexity according to state and jurisdiction) and the implications for the profession:

- **Fiscal crises**: Public sector fiscal crises due to the built-in structural deficits in many states and the federal government.

- **Demographic changes**: changes over the next two decades reflecting an increasingly aging baby boomer population and a "truly pluralistic, multicultural society."

- **The impact of technology**, particularly social media's impact, on community engagement and service delivery.

- **Increasingly polarized politics** at the local level reflect the national dynamic.

- The increasing **gap between the have and have-nots**.

The environment described by Bob O'Neill requires multisector, multidisciplinary, and intergovernmental strategies if there is to be any hope of solving difficult problems that transcend boundaries. The larger national and international contexts in which cities and counties are embedded are dominated by constant change, where the new normal is no longer risk management but risk containment—it is no longer controlling budgets but making constant budget adjustments. The competencies required now include agility and flexibility, specifically the willingness and desire to solve complex problems in an interdependent way when the outcomes are uncertain and ambiguous.

Current Context Variables

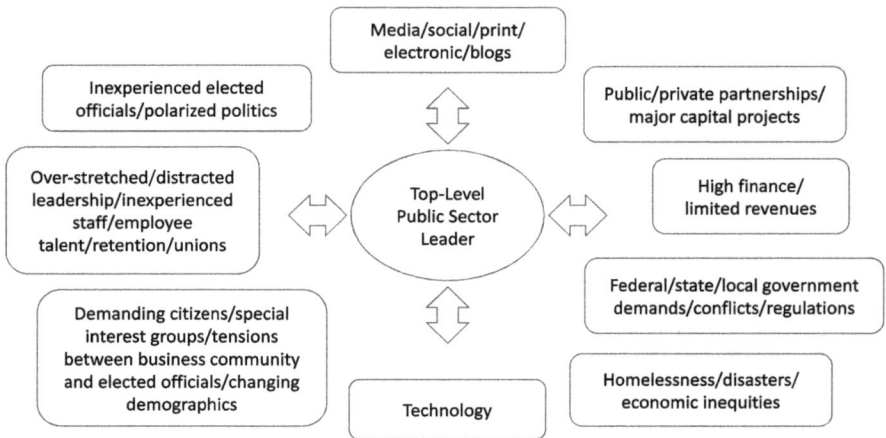

Diagram: *"Current Context Variables"* at play in the public sector. *Utilizing content analysis, these are the typical complexities identified in the local environment that face top-level public sector leaders.* © *Sopp, T., 2007; updated, 2020.*

Current Context Variables

Current context variables are the day-to-day realities top-level public sector leaders faced over the years during my research across many types of public organizations. Within the larger national and international environment and the public sector environment the ICMA described, the *local* current context for city and county managers might look like the diagram above.

Starting at the top of the diagram, moving clockwise, local and national **media/social media, blogs, and internet community activity** create an immediate and reactive cycle for managerial staff, boards, and elected officials. Devoting attention to the latest posts on X, Instagram, TikTok, Facebook, or blog posts takes up an enormous amount of time and creates distracted leaders. While it is easy to argue that technology has simply made information more democratic, the focus here is on technology's ability to be a distraction.

Distracted leaders do not serve communities well. It takes a great deal of self-discipline on the part of top-level public sector leaders and their staff to resist the tendency to want to address the latest critique immediately, using available technologies. This behind-the-scenes action takes time away from the delivery of core services or important priority initiatives. Furthermore, this type of dynamic creates an environment ripe for a misjudgment or misstep due to time pressures to respond immediately versus taking a day or two to make a considered response. For example, reactive behaviors might include initially hindering transparency due to the need to check with others before responding, not being forthcoming with all the information, acting defensively, speaking out of turn before all the facts are collected, and acting in ways that create a spiral of action and reaction. This dynamic creates winners and losers rather quickly and requires more politically astute response skills. As a result of social media activity, this reactive environment is now a persistent reality for top-level public sector leaders, and their staff are essentially required to respond to posts on X or citizen-generated blog posts explaining the city, county, or special district's actions, anticipate how to get out in front of a news story with tweets of their own, and actively participate with equal fervor in this increasingly demanding communication responsibility. Thus, this environment is a perfect stage for missteps.

Public/private partnerships and capital projects inevitably bring scrutiny, complexity, and mistakes. They require expertise in dealing with *high financing* issues, sometimes also referred to as "creative financing," and these partnerships with the private sector can result in value conflicts. Some projects that have resulted in conflicts include the building of a ballpark, the construction of a hotel near an arts center, and the provision of contracts for affordable housing. The pressure to negotiate like the private sector, to cut corners to meet deadlines, and to do "whatever it takes to get it done" because elected officials are counting on a ribbon-cutting ceremony within the timeframe of their term has created demands that are not easily finessed within the confines of public sector norms. Even if no one has done anything illegal or for personal gain, the visibility of a project often leads to supervisors or staff at various levels being replaced or moved. Reputations can be negatively impacted, and sometimes, those at the top are sacrificed if they are considered to be blocking progress on the project or being a stickler about the details or rules. Taking on a visible capital project requires a set of financial, technical, and political skills that are of the highest level and can be a career-enhancing or career-ending experience.

Federal, state, and local governments alike have been demanding housing for the homeless population and affordable housing mandates; infrastructure improvements, such as for stormwater and flood management; new redevelopment policies; and regulations to reduce emissions and pollutants, to name a few. However, they have provided little or no money accompanying these mandates. The financial management skills required to find room in the budget to cover these mandates and still deliver on the initiatives or services promised by elected officials to their constituents are often impossible to achieve. This pressure, again, creates an environment that heightens the tension about budget decision-making within a context of structural deficits at the state and federal levels. This is an additional complexity to an already tight budget for local governments.

Environmental, economic, political, and social service issues have also added to the complexity of the environments in which public leaders work. In that same article by Bob O'Neill, the ICMA identified an increasingly built-in have/have not dynamic that has developed in local government communities. This political division reflects the national bifurcation stemming from changing demographics in age, race, and ethnicity, as well as changing definitions of equality, equity, and diversity, which means changing values. The list of issues is long and includes some of the following:

- Homelessness and affordable housing;

- Well-documented racial inequalities in police protection and health care inequalities recently exposed and publicized by current social justice movements;

- Climate change which has contributed to disasters like the chronic fires in some states like California, Washington, New Mexico, Nevada, and Utah; energy issues resulting in power grid blackouts in Texas; the heightened impact of floods throughout the country; increasingly destructive snow storms in the east; and water shortages in the western states.

- Political terrorism or the threat of terrorism in the forms of both warfare and cyberterrorism, as well as the rise of terrorist groups within the United States.

This complex environment has also increased the amount of bad citizen behavior, where the public is defying rules/regulations that were previously honored. For example, a rather nonpolitical but telling set of behaviors perpetrated by the public occurred in 2019 in the City of Lake Elsinore, California.[4] An overwhelming number of citizens ignored the posted signs not to step off the path in Walker Canyon, where the wildflowers were blooming. Social media had taken over and drew locals and visitors to the wildflowers. Troves of cars and citizens/guests to the city defied the rules, stopped their cars on the freeway to take pictures, stepped off the canyon paths, and trampled over the wildflowers while taking selfies. One city worker was hit by a car as a result of collisions that occurred because cars were parked on the freeway as their passengers were trying to gain quick access to the wildflowers. The park staff were completely unprepared for this behavior, as it had never occurred before, and they had to quickly create guidelines and figure out how to route the crowds and transport them out safely. A year later, the city was ready, but because of a lack of rainfall related to climate change, there were no blooming wildflowers in 2020 or 2021.

This occurrence exemplifies that the world of top-level public sector leaders often involves managing changing values, behaviors, and trends that reflect the larger environment.

Technology has created an environment where local governments are expected to be transparent, responsive to an increasing number of public record requests, and adaptable, as they must address privacy issues around data and data analytics that come with smart streetlights, license plate readers, and other developments like artificial intelligence (AI). Questions surrounding what data to collect and how to use the data have been asked, and the role of the community in this decision-making process has been questioned as well. For example, is it legitimate to use drones for code enforcement? The ever-changing environment surrounding technology and innovation can easily catch the city or county off guard in their response to the implications of using the latest technologies. Alternatively, perceived misjudgments may result in ripple effects on justice issues, such as in the use of smart streetlights. Simply scratching at the surface of a controversy facing a public sector leader right now would likely reveal its root in a new technology dilemma.

Demanding citizen groups and an active chamber of commerce are bringing more lawsuits, initiatives for the ballot box, and business community pushbacks against elected officials. For example, in 2018, the Seattle business community actively targeted five council member seats and the mayor's office in an effort to overturn an unpopular tax increase.[5] Given the changing demographic groups that are increasingly wanting to be seen and acknowledged, an aging population, and a changing majority group or the dissolution of any majority groups, top-level public sector leaders are increasingly having to manage these dynamics.

Overstretched experienced staff are delegating to less experienced staff and sometimes promoting them to positions they are unprepared to assume. Inexperienced staff tend to respond quickly and can have knee-jerk reactions to citizen complaints. Often, they lack knowledge of the history of the players involved in a particular city, county, or water agency project, how this project was viewed by the public in the past, and the landmines that had been previously stepped in or avoided. They often lack the finesse or savvy needed to navigate internal and external organizational politics and may miss the political interests involved altogether. Mistakes are made, and these missteps land on the top-level public leader's desk.

Additionally, there have been unexpected talent pool issues, given the lower wages in the public sector, the increasing lack of interest in working in the public sector, ripple effects of the mass exodus of the workforce seen nationwide, legitimate pressures for a skills-first approach to hiring, and employee demands for remote/hybrid work that is a permanent arrangement. Regarding labor issues, there are increasing pressures and demands for reforms and benefits by labor unions, as their influence is back on the rise. These demands are felt most acutely by city and county managers and elected officials. If the public sector organization is in a state where unions have made sizable campaign contributions and/or endorsed the campaigns of council members, mayors, and elected officials at the county or state level, this adds additional pressure to the top-level public leader's role.

Polarized politics among city councils, county boards of supervisors, and elected regional boards often reflect the state-level or national polarization of politics.[6] As one generation of elected and appointed public officials passes the baton to another, the more inexperienced elected officials question, blog about, and challenge the status quo, both to the benefit and detriment of public policy decisions. More socially progressive new members tend to question the status quo, and then the cycle becomes that more conservative new members challenge past practices as well.

Mandatory term limits on the length of time a local- or state-level elected official can serve have exacerbated this issue of inexperience and created a never-ending cycle of new players. Often, just when the players are coming to trust and understand each other and learning how to navigate the process from policy to implementation, a new player is elected due to term limits. Water boards are particularly impacted by polarized politics because term limits came late to water agencies, and only now are they beginning to be instituted. This movement of new board members onto previously unchanged boards and the relationships that go with these moves have a significant impact on the public agency leader's role in handling tensions and trust issues. Relationships are often the glue that helps make the work of policy implementation possible, and the institution of term limits puts a strain on these long-standing relationships.

The picture that is being painted for you here details the context in which missteps and scandals happen. They are not simply the result of the personal character flaw of a city manager, county administrator, or other high-level public sector leader. To reiterate, the misstep may, in fact, be an ethical blind spot of the leader, and this blind spot can be sparked into a full blown scandal by these contexts. That is, the context in which the behavior occurs contributes to the missteps we see from the outside. It is critically important for any top-level public sector leader to understand the complex set of factors so that they become exceptionally aware of their environmental context so that they may become even more vigilant of their behavior. Top-level public sector leaders must be on watch for these variables at all times.

Current Structural Arrangements Variables

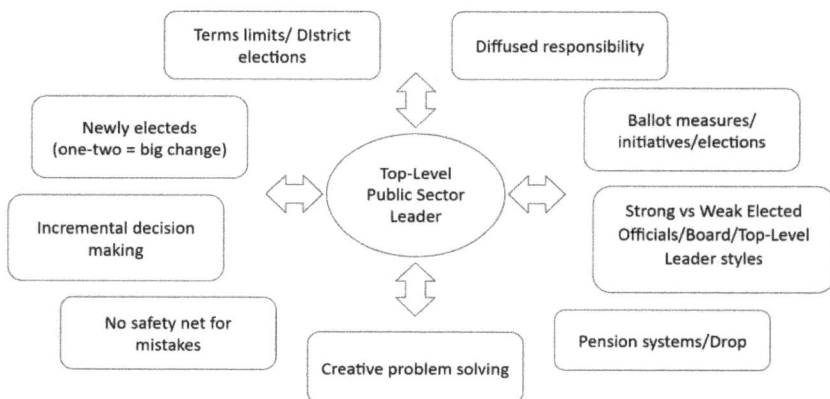

Diagram: "Current Structural Arrangements Variables" at play in the public sector. Utilizing content analysis, these are the typical complexities identified in the environment that top-level public sector leaders have less control over but must manage. ©Sopp, T., 2007; updated, 2020.

Current Structural Arrangements Variables

There are also current structural arrangements that top-level public sector leaders must deal with. That is, they must account for those variables that were built into the structure of the government—structures over which they have no control. The top-level leader inherits these structures by virtue of the position they occupy, and these structures impact and sometimes drive the leader's behavior. These structural arrangements are detailed in the diagram above.

Starting at the top left of the diagram and moving clockwise, variable **term limits** have created a never-ending succession of new elected officials who often operate with a short-term, four-to-eight-year mentality. As such, they apply pressure for quick fixes. These quick fixes may help honor election promises or build a good resume for elected officials' future careers, but they can often create long-term problems for future administrations. Coupled with term limits, **district elections** create a dynamic in which the elected official is primarily wearing the hat of their district versus assessing the city or county as a whole. Consequently, they might be making decisions based only on what is best for their district, and their decisions might be different if they were to consider a city-wide or county-wide perspective. The full impact of this approach is not known, as there is little longitudinal data or research on this topic. A long-held argument, and a recently created legal requirement in some cities, is to transition to district elections to ensure better representation for underserved and disadvantaged communities.

Regardless of the purpose and reason for district elections, an election is a procedure that impacts the dynamics of the elected body or board and the community at large. It also impacts the daily lives of top-level public leaders, such as city administrators.

Depending on the size of the organization, the people doing the work may be situated, **diffused in responsibility**, several levels away from the purview of the top-level public sector leader and may not feel the weight of responsibility for decisions and actions due to the compartmentalization of tasks. What comes with diffused responsibility is often an increased lack of ownership over ethical dilemmas as a result of not having the full picture and/or a lack of feeling of any accountability for the consequences of the decisions made.[7] It is unclear how the new arrangement of remote work impacts this dynamic of diffused responsibility. The distance becomes not about the hierarchical distance between the levels but the physical distance resulting from communication through Zoom, Microsoft Teams, or Google Chat rather than face-to-face meetings, field "tailgate" meetings, or drop-in conversations.

Role conflicts stem from the built-in structural arrangement between the top-level public sector leader and the elected official decision-making body (i.e., city council or board of supervisors). For example, in municipal government environments a **strong council/strong mayor style** that steps over the line into the operational domain of the city manager can create difficulties and confusion among city staff, especially if they try to direct staff. This is different from the voter-approached strong mayor form of government described in Chapter One. In the case described here, it is the personality and style of the city council and mayor that is "strong," not the voter-approved structure referred to as the "strong mayor." Conversely, a **weak city council/weak mayor style**, which is where the council and/or mayor drags their feet or won't make important and timely policy decisions, could cause a city manager to step in and fill the void. This style is also ripe for a **strong city manager style** that steps over the line into the arena of policymaking, which is the arena of the city council and mayor, not the city manager. The consequences are many if this dynamic occurs at a city, county, or water agency board level. While the line between policy and operations can be blurry at the highest levels, and some would argue that this is a false distinction entirely, there are clear role differences. Deviating too much from these roles creates confusion at all levels. Whatever direction this confusion takes, it can create a shadow government for the city, county, or water agency outside the appropriate roles approved by the organization's charter. This becomes another structural issue for top-level public sector leaders to manage.

The growing **pension obligations**[8] faced by public agencies can create budget headaches every year. When this variable is combined with the structural deficits that many state governments face, the headache becomes one to be managed and absorbed by top-level public sector leaders. Pension reform initiatives within agencies or by citizen groups have contributed to a constant gray cloud that hangs over the recruitment and retention of public sector employees.

Retirement incentive programs can aid in the retention of experienced employees who provide wonderful mentoring opportunities for the organization or continue in specialized positions that allow the organization more time to recruit or develop replacements. However, there can also be unintended consequences. For example, through one big city's Deferred Retirement Option Program (DROP), employees can officially retire and lock in their retirement income on the books but continue working in their positions and receiving their regular salary for up to five years. Their retirement income is held in a special account that earns interest, and it is made available to them once they leave. A few unintended consequences have occurred, such as unhappy employees staying longer than they might have intended and their lingering low morale impacting their teams. Additionally, a top-level leader's influence may have waned, and their ineffectiveness or lack of influence might hamper the team throughout their DROP program years. Another example is that higher-level employees may stay longer, blocking the promotion of other employees (see Chapter Five, "Notes" section for a further explanation and description of DROP). This is a legal, negotiated benefit, and it takes enormous effort and political will, short of a bankruptcy scenario, for the top-level public sector leader and city council to challenge or change it. All the while, it is a structural variable that impacts their organizations in concrete ways.

Norms are structures, and role relationships are powerful structures. Consequently, the unspoken norm and perception believed by city councils, boards of supervisors, and/or water agency boards is that the top-level public sector leader has all the answers, knows everything, and has the solution to everything. Thus, norms have a powerful impact on the day-to-day reality of top-level leaders. The mantra "Don't tell me what I can't do; tell me what I can do" is rewarded and brings kudos, but this has consequences. It creates a repetitive cycle of demands and can create pressure on public leaders to do some risky and **creative problem-solving** to deliver on projects and requests made by their elected officials.

Furthermore, there is **no safety net for mistakes**. The 24/7 news cycle means that there is no time to regroup without being in the spotlight. This is a painful reality that is punishing. There is little reward for honesty other than the ethical satisfaction and model this sets for employees, although getting in front of a scandal or mistake can limit the time and attention it gets. And, from the perspective of the elected official, there's pressure on the top-level leader to keep mistakes from going public.

Structurally, governance often consists of piecemeal, **incremental decision-making** and is not holistic. One short-term decision is followed by another, then another, and another so that problems are not always completely solved but instead recur. These quick fixes can often fail immediately or over time, and then the question becomes, "Who do we blame for this?" or "How did we get here in the first place, and who made that decision?" Often, this cycle of blame creates an atmosphere where information flow shuts down, risks are minimized, a lack of information leads to poor problem-solving, and more mistakes occur.

With the election cycles, a **new set of council or board members** may be installed who are not as committed to the top-level public sector manager they inherit. This changes the power dynamics for a period of time and may even cause top-level leaders to lose their jobs.

Summary Remarks

Top-level public sector leaders face staggering complexity in their work environments. There is the larger political, economic, environmental, and social environment of the state, nation, and world at large that impacts the local government agency, city, and county. There are the nine current context issues outlined, which includes the media, dangers inherent in public/private partnerships, requirements imposed by governmental entities at all levels, social issues, and the impact of technology on civic participation and expectations, all of which have an impact on the local government. Demanding citizen groups, demographic changes, and talent pool problems that lead to inexperienced staff are further examples of contextual issues.

Furthermore, the polarization of politics at the national level is reflected in the behavior of local boards and councils. On top of this are nine immovable structural arrangements variables such as term limits for elected officials, the diffused responsibility of roles, potential role conflicts between strong/weak councils and mayors, and strong/weak city managers. Pension obligations are a structural deficit inherent in public agencies. They create pressure to solve problems instantly with quick fixes, a spotlight environment where mistakes are magnified, and pressure to make decisions incrementally versus focusing on the root cause. There is also added insecurity from the constant turnover in elected officials due to term limits. Therefore, the council or board that hires an official might not be the same council or board the official might work for down the line.

All these variables are simultaneously interacting and influencing each other. When a top-level public sector leader ignores or underestimates the context in which they work, they will underestimate the actions, solutions, and extraordinary sensors they need to mitigate the ethical issues, putting their careers and reputations in peril. Going out on top requires that leaders' peripheral vision be fixed on all of these variables, including those in the next chapters -personal characteristics and blind spots.

Endnotes

[1] See Schmantes (2019) and Gottfried (2019) for discussions of prior research on gossip in the workplace.

[2] Citation source confidential. See Appendix B for all articles referencing missteps, misjudgments, or scandals.

[3] See O'Neill (2013). Other writings on complexity in the public sector include Kuehne (2021), Murphy et al. (2016), and Ho (2012).

[4] See Schwartz (2019) and Schaben (2019). I conducted an informal interview with Grant Yates, former city manager of the City of Lake Elsinore, on March, 28, 2022.

[5] Semuels (2019).

[6] O'Neill (2013).

[7] Trevino & Nelson (2017), pp. 283–284.

[8] For a chart on typical public pension burdens facing city governments, see *Paradise Plundered*, by S. Erie (2011), p. 94. Other helpful articles include Walter (2020), Yadavall (2019), and Lenney et al. (2021).

Chapter Three

Personal Factors that Impact Judgment and Behavior

Top-level public sector leaders approach their positions with their own personal beliefs or ways of thinking, mindsets, and a specific set of skills that impact their judgment and behavior. This is in addition to the current context and structural arrangements they face, as detailed in Chapter Two. These professional and personal beliefs, mindsets, and skills are factors that top-level leaders can control because they can adopt different ways of thinking, change their beliefs, and improve their skills. Even though these factors are more flexible than the current context and structural arrangements, they are powerful internal *structures* that influence individual actions. That is, they frame the way leaders process what they experience in their roles and how they behave.

For example, if the top-level public sector leader essentially trusts others' intent before evidence to the contrary (a personal or professional belief formed over time), is a good listener and non-defensive in their communication style (a skill), and is clear and consistent about the responsibilities of their role as an administrator and not a politician (a mindset), they bring these structures to the table as they execute their role. Another example, albeit extreme, might be a top-level public sector leader who is suspicious of others and assumes that at all times self-interest is at play (a personal or professional belief), is quick to judge and debate in their communication style, hearing critique as an attack (a communication skill style), and believes that their role is to pursue a certain agenda about a policy or operational matter because the elected officials keep getting it wrong, and in their administrative role, they engage in subtle battle to prove they are correct even to the extent that they might allow certain projects to fail to prove a point (a mindset). One can surmise how these very different leadership beliefs, mindsets, and skills might yield different outcomes. I have seen these behaviors in various combinations, and they are *structures* as powerful as any context or structural variable.

Personal Factors that Impact Judgment and Behavior

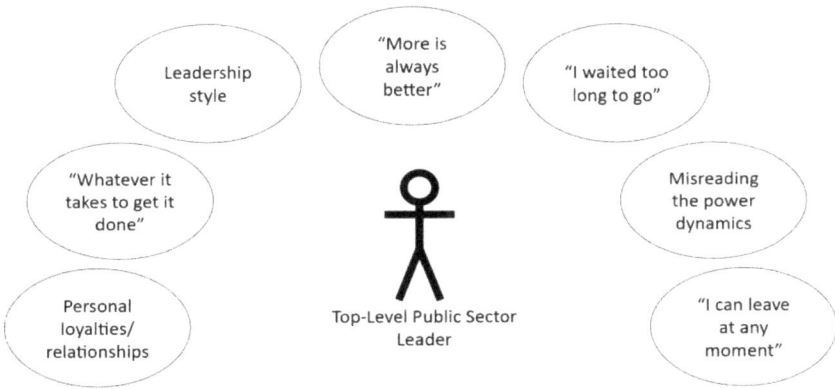

Diagram: "Personal Factors that Impact Judgment and Behavior" are the personal beliefs, mindsets, and skills that top-level public leaders hold that impact their judgment and behavior. This model was developed utilizing a methodology of grounded theory and content analysis. Patterns were identified and labeled.© Sopp, T., 2020.

These beliefs, mindsets, and skills are personal factors and they influence and impact every employee below the top-level leader and certainly impact those they report to—the elected officials.

There are seven characteristics outlined moving from left to right along the arch.

Personal Loyalty or Relationships

Something that evolves over time is the **personal loyalty or relationships** that top-level public sector leaders typically form with the elected officials, mayor, and/or board chair under whom they serve. This is usually rooted in the belief that it is the top-level public sector leader's responsibility to deliver for the mayor, board chair, and/or elected officials, to serve the vision/policy direction represented by these officials, and to help them create a stellar legacy and achieve a particular set of goals for the citizenry at large. The elected officials determine the direction, and the top-level leader drives the ship in that direction. The loyalty this symbiotic relationship creates tends to cause the top-level public leader to stay longer in the position than they, or their family, perhaps want simply because the mayor or chair of the board desires it.

For example, perhaps the chair of the board wants the top-level leader to help with the chair's legacy projects, or perhaps the union president needs the top-level leader to help with upcoming labor negotiations because this leader is especially trusted by the labor groups, but the timelines for these projects fall outside the leader's desire to stay in the position. Another example might be that the chamber of commerce pressures the top-level public sector leader behind the scenes to stay longer for the good of the city and business interests; they might say, "Just until we get a new city council...." One retired top-level public sector leader, Mr. Wise and Noble Leader, said it more starkly: "Elected officials think they own you." He additionally remarked that he was asked, "What would it cost (us) for you to stay?" with the implication being that no cost is too high.[1] There is powerful pressure to respond to the needs of elected officials once they count on you. Personal loyalty or relationships can cloud the top-level public sector leader's best judgment, as the public leader might ignore or discount their own personal desires, career interests, or sense that it is time to go.

"Whatever it takes to get it done."

The mentality that some top-level public sector leaders can develop over time, especially when time is short and pressure is high, is the **"whatever it takes to get it done"** mindset. This message is heard loud and clear by staff, permeates the organization, and creates shortcut behaviors that can yield sloppy results and inevitably lead to trouble. This norm usually develops and stays as a consequence of capital projects that go over the budget. Furthermore, they might receive some public attention through the media, and the pressure to deliver is on the elected official(s), which means it is on the top-level leader, managers, and supervisors below. The more expensive the project, the more pressure there is on timelines. The more scrutiny there is, the more pressure there is on the leader to create a successful ending. This might mean that the top-level public sector leader needs to cut corners to achieve the relevant goals.

An example of the "whatever it takes to get it done" pressure is one of big city's Real Estate Deals. The property, a former energy agency's vacant high-rise headquarters, was dictated by a lease-to-own agreement approved by the city council in January 2017. The purpose of the acquisition was to move existing city staff into the available and vacant high-rise building to save on leasing costs, as city staff were working out of several different buildings throughout downtown and other sites in the city. A few years after the building was leased, stories appeared in the press that the building was still vacant while just over $500,000 per month of rent was being paid. As public perception worsened and political pressure mounted, staff were moved in after some renovations were completed.

Some insiders saw the move into the building as premature, given that the renovations disrupted preexisting asbestos and triggered inspections by county code enforcement staff. They speculated that the move occurred quickly after renovations to save the mayor from the embarrassment of the media coverage surrounding the cost per day of the delay. The entire project, from the selection and the lease-to-own agreement to the role lobbyists, might have played in the deal, the site's renovation, the premature move into the building, and the consequent exit after two weeks, was audited and investigated. While litigation was pending, a settlement was reached between the parties. What still remains to be seen is litigation from city staff who might have been exposed to asbestos because the building was not yet ready for occupation. Whatever comes of the remaining litigation, the big city's Real Estate Deal, even with the recent settlement, has been labeled by the community and citizens as a poor decision, scandal, and debacle.

When it is at play, the "whatever it takes to get it done" mindset is not an innocuous mentality.

Leadership Style

The **leadership style** of the top-level public sector leader and their skills, experience, and temperament set the organizational tone as to how problems are solved and how best to communicate up to elected officials and down to staff. These attributes dictate how the top-level leader navigates the rules, norms, or previously identified contexts or structural arrangements. The leadership style that top-level leaders adopt influences the perspective they take to solve problems, and this perspective ripples throughout the organization, regardless of its size.

A balanced and healthy leadership style fosters the growth and development of staff, is calm and calculated when dealing with ambiguous situations, and is measured and mature when addressing conflict situations. Problematic leadership styles get the leader and the organization, by extension, in trouble. For example, if the top-level public sector leader is conflict-averse, they are likely to seek solutions that avoid conflict, which will often involve superficial fixes. It would be difficult to overstate how consequential a top-level public sector leader's risk tolerance is to the tone and culture of the organization. How risk is defined, modeled, and rewarded speaks volumes up to the elected officials and down to the staff. If they can't tolerate ambiguity, they rush to fix problems quickly. This results in a lot of activity and a lot of changes in direction to decrease the tension that ambiguous situations create. If leaders are eager to please elected officials and deliver on all their requests, the ripple effects on the organization are often an overworked staff, conflicting priorities, the over-committing of resources, and subtle resistance from the ranks.

A decision-making style that is overly inclusive or overly commanding and controlling is equally problematic and inefficient, and the best decisions aren't being made because too many people, or not the right people, are in the room. A communication style where the leader keeps critical information to themselves and relinquishes it only

46

when they think it is time or perhaps never does but uses it solely for their own purposes has ripple effects as well. These effects create a bottleneck in decision-making because, consequently, no one in their chain of command would be well informed, disenabling the making of informed decisions. Imagine this occurring as an accidental side effect of a poor communicator, and then imagine this happening intentionally when the top-level public sector leader might be doing battle with the elected officials. What do you suppose the reaction of the elected body might be when they realize, over time, that the operational staff are consistently not informed or briefed or consulted with by their top-level public sector leader? Or that select operational staff may have intentionally been kept out of the loop about requests from the elected official so that the elected official's favorite project fades away or fails? Or that critical information that only staff has, has been withheld at the direction of the top-level leader?

These illustrate just a few problematic styles in action. The point is that leadership and decision-making styles create a prism through which actions are taken and can foster or limit staff performance. Leadership characteristics like beliefs, mindsets, and skills **contribute to a climate in which missteps happen**. They profoundly impact the tone that is set in the organization, whether the information is passed on, and whether the right risks or any risks are taken.

In every community, there are both citizens who can't take no for an answer and elected officials who won't take no for an answer. This translates into a dilemma for the top-level public sector leader in terms of how to respond: Is there a bottom line? Is there a limit to accommodating an unreasonable request? Is there a clear moral compass dictating what is right or wrong? Does that compass move so much that the line distinguishing accommodation and wrongful behavior becomes blurred? Is there a natural desire to please (which most public servants have) and defer or absorb bad news or always find a way to make something work, no matter the impact on staff? Can this issue be solved another way, and is the time to do so feasible? How these dilemmas are addressed is a window into any top-level public sector leader's leadership style, and the values and characteristics of this style impact the organization, as staff at all levels are watching and getting their cues on how to handle situations from the top-level leader.

"More is always better."

The topic of personal mindsets like **"more is always better"** is a more delicate subject. That is, what the top-level public sector leader brings to the table is deeply personal and reflects the human frailties we all have. What is discussed in the following paragraphs can have a particularly direct impact on the careers of top-level public sector leaders.

The mindset that **"more is always better"** is akin to Collins' (2009) cautionary tale regarding the "undisciplined pursuit of more."[2] For example, this can manifest as the top-level public sector leader being overly responsive to council members and their wish lists, regardless of whether the proposed projects are manageable or feasible. The top-level leader might operate under the belief that some activity is better than no activity or that saying no is not an option because of the conflict or negative consequences this might bring. There is no question that elected officials can bring about this "more is always better" mindset with the unspoken sentiment they often feel: "What have you done for me lately?" Elected officials want a resume of accomplishments around which to base their campaigns, and the top-level public sector leader is central to ensuring that these accomplishments are achieved. It is difficult for top-level leaders to refrain from constantly being responsive to every request made by their elected bodies, independent of a critical review by themselves or staff.

Something else that influences this mindset includes when the top-level public sector leader becomes impatient or bored in the role they occupy. They may take on riskier projects to stay interested or make the city or county more of a high-profile presence in the news as a result. They might also fill their plates with projects happening at the same time to stay busy and avoid personal problems. Furthermore, they might compete with another city/county agency just to even a score from a several-year-old slight or sabotage something as important as merging two central library institutions together for the sake of efficiency. These personal frailties or human dimensions of top-level leaders can play themselves out and create the very environment that leads to a serious misstep.

Some top-level public sector leaders want to deliver on the wish list of requests from elected officials and their constituents so much that they can't see or deny the risks inherent in a flawed project. Consequently, they may stall or never deliver the bad news that this current course of action is not the right direction to take. Denial of the risk built into a project can lead to actions that make the error even worse. For example, a top-level public sector leader of a medium-sized city recounted a story during a leadership academy in which the council had approved a high-profile infrastructure project to deliver on a promise to the community. However, the staff knew the project was faulty even when it was approved. Eventually, the planning and engineering departments spoke up and told the top-level public sector leader that it was not a good idea to continue spending on this project, that the project had never been a good idea, that the costs had been misrepresented, that this project was not going to work out as planned, and that it would actually be a hazard. The groundbreaking ceremony had already taken place, and a fair amount of money had already been spent, so there was surely criticism to come from the community.

If this top-level public sector leader had not been so secure in his position as a result of the goodwill garnered after years of fulfilling the council's wishes, and if this leader had not had the confidence that he could handle the conflict and recriminations that would ensue, as well as the character to know what his bottom line was in this situation, this information may have been withheld from the council or, once learned, may have led to the dismissal of the leader. As it turned out, the top-level public sector leader reported the facts to the city council in a public forum and the mistake the leader and staff had made in recommending it. While there were media headlines critiquing the top-level public sector leader and staff, there was also praise for the top-level public sector leader for being transparent about the mistake. [3]That praise softened the community blowback for the elected body.

The character of the top-level public sector leader matters. Character strengths related to telling the truth, facing risk honestly, and not falling into the trap of "more is always better" cannot be underestimated as a key factor in a leader's career success. These personal leadership characteristics, i.e., beliefs, mindsets, and skills that the top-level leader brings to the table, can contribute to the complex reasons behind why missteps or scandals happen and are key to when they are avoided.

"I waited too long to go…"

A big regret of many top-level public sector leaders is often that **"I waited too long to go…I wanted to leave but stayed (then bad things happened)."** Given the complexity of the environment outlined in previous chapters, it is guaranteed that bad things will eventually happen in a top-level public sector leader's career. For many leaders believe **"it is honorable to stay"** and not depart when dark clouds are on the horizon. Or the top-level leader just procrastinates because some days are good and some are bad, and it doesn't get bad enough to leave, but they know it could, and then it does, and they are stuck in the position when bad things happen. The mantra they recite to themselves, "I am in it for the long run; I am devoted to this mayor", is too simplistic. While it is legitimate for leaders to hold the belief that they are experienced and skilled enough to weather the storm, it is also possible that leaders' perspectives and presence have contributed to the storm. Saving the organization from the pain of watching their leader get thrown under the bus has advantages, too. It is a difficult calculus and one worth debating and contemplating rather than dismissing out of hand.

Misreading the Power Dynamics

Closely related to the "denial of risk" error that is covered in Chapter Four, "Blind Spots That Lead to Errors in Judgment", is **misreading the power dynamics** in an organization. This error can be subdivided into several smaller errors, which are informed by various mindsets.

While coaching a top-level public sector leader who had received any number of subtle and not-so-subtle messages that her performance and demeanor were not meeting expectations, she said during the coaching session, "I am committed to this organization, and I have no intention of leaving."[4] The mindset she carried around was, "I can handle any role or problem, no matter the players involved." This stance of hers was completely inaccurate. It ignored the fact that she had lost influence with several important players in the organization, and it ignored the tension her presence created and the impact this had on the department, as well as the reputation of her department within the organization. She had grown ineffective.[5]

The emotional intelligence (EQ) that top-level public sector jobs require is considerable. It is a high bar to be self-aware of what triggers us, know how to self-manage reactions, recognize how others are feeling, and work to create a sustainable, long-lasting network of relationships, as well as to do all of this within a broader political environment. If top-level public sector leaders' self-management or relationship-building skills are not fully developed, they could easily succumb to the pitfall of overlooking the power dynamics at play in their organizational or community contexts. Perhaps the leader moved up too quickly and was unaware of who was in or out, how information is currency, how to use expert power but that likability matters as much or more, or how taking sides or being vocal about personal opinions over the years can get them in trouble once they assume the top position. For example, a big city's city manager shared with me that the difference between being the assistant city manager and the city manager was like night and day. The top-level public sector leader's *environment* is nearly completely political, no matter the size of the organization, and many in these positions may initially be unprepared for this reality and the self-awareness this reality requires. While the role is administrative and operational, the political environment the top-level leader resides in (i.e., reporting to an elected body) requires a savvy understanding, appreciation, and awareness of the interests of all parties.

There is a seriousness to overlooking the power dynamics or missing the clues in your organization. Adopting the mindset that you are self-aware enough or that "I can handle any role or problem no matter the players involved" is a career-ending mistake if you are wrong. If you think you are self-aware, but you are not, or if you think you have a handle on your triggers but you do not, this is certainly a form of hubris that is at the root of many ethical blind spots. Additionally, there are certainly ethics involved in the impact that immature abilities related to EQ may have on staff. However, my focus here is not on ethics per se— it is on the dangerous pattern I am seeing of too many leaders seriously unaware of their triggers and the impact this has on their management behavior and decisions.

Recently, I watched several top-level public sector leaders in both big and medium-sized cities, and a medium-sized RTA, seek coaching expertise for themselves. They questioned and challenged the feedback they received, tried to find out who said what about them rather than focusing on the validity of the data, and became argumentative with others whom they believed may have passed along a critique of them. They wanted to prove the person giving the feedback was wrong and rationalized any decisions or actions they took that had a negative impact on others as "that's okay, my job is to shake things up."[6]

Noonan's 2007 book, *Discussing the Undiscussable: A Guide to Overcoming Defensive Routines,*[7] wrote about defensive routines in organizations, that is, "patterns of interpersonal interactions that people create to protect themselves from embarrassment or threat," and these behaviors certainly qualify as such. The principles of EQ argue that this is a lack of self-awareness and self-management, which strikes me as a huge understatement. My concern is that this is precisely the behavior that causes staff to go underground, stand on the sidelines, and simply wait and hide out until the bad things that are going to happen do in fact happen. This behavior is an example of missing the clues, missing the power dynamics, and replacing good questions of inquiry and good dialogue with "got you" defensive routines. Rather than improving organizations, these attacking behaviors send people underground, and problems don't get solved. Instead, they recur, and then there are missteps, misjudgments, and scandals. Information freezes in an environment of blame, and good, competent information is required to solve problems.

The final mindset that falls under misreading the power dynamics is that "results are what matters, not how people feel." Many top-level public sector leaders can get caught up in the task of fulfilling their elected officials' wish lists and delivering results quickly, irrespective of the impact on the staff. Often, the belief of the leader is that the reward is the work and satisfaction with a job well done, but the psychic reward for staff is generally not as tangible as the psychic reward the leader receives from the elected official by fulfilling the list of requests over and over again. "Pulling it off" requires resources and staff muscle. Thus, this mindset often leads to a misreading of the power dynamics **downward**, that is, how a leader's behavior and pace impacts the department directors or other mid-level managers below. I have watched many newly appointed top-level leaders pile on projects and say "yes" to all requests, only to fuel a silent rebellion that builds up among directors who feel overworked and unsupported, as they are left critically lacking the resources to pull it off. A leader's insensitivity to their impact, a misreading of the delicate and complex balance of power between other levels and players below, can create perspectives at the top that are inaccurate or not reflective of what others may need from leaders. Leaders can't "pull it off" without the staff below, and the staff below can slow down and refuse to cooperate in ways leaders might not be able to imagine. The "do it for me" mentality can only last so long, and if leaders consistently take more than they give, there are consequences.

"I can leave at any moment."

Overly comfortable with one year left or past their retirement age, leaders with the "I can leave at any moment, and they (elected officials) know that" mindset can veer toward carelessness. The comfort with this mindset may help the leader at a personal level by allowing them to sleep better at night. However, it can also seep into day-to-day decision-making that may feel cavalier to staff, especially when it comes to decisions and actions where the stakes are high for those who plan to stay with the organization for many more years.

Mr. Controversial Visionary, the big city's RTA leader who was recruited and hired about a year after the previous leader, Mr. Charisma, resigned after the scandal around the financial projections (see Chapter One case study), remarked that his vision for the next three years was either going to make him a "hero or he would go out in a blazing crash-and-burn scenario." This can make for a daring, once-in-a-lifetime opportunity that can propel an organization forward or leave years of cleanup for those left behind. However, at the time of our consultation, Mr. Controversial Visionary was potentially misreading, or overly optimistic, about the direction the political winds might eventually take, the increasing complexity of the environment in which he resided, and the votes that were required to pull off his vision, which were not there. All of this ultimately left the organization with no satisfactory backup plan. This mentality could change with new leadership, an abrupt change in circumstance, and/or a new board.

In another example, the mindset of "I can leave at any moment" can foster a healthy desire to take risks or even a level of comfort that enables frank conversations with elected officials when the occasion requires. If overdone, the opposite—unhealthy risk-taking—occurs. When unhealthy risk-taking and a mindset of prioritizing "whatever it takes to get it done" take hold in an engineering or utilities department, some serious shortcuts can result, and these can easily lead to a misstep, lapse in judgment, or scandal.

The question here is, does the mental model of "I can leave at any moment" create a dynamic where the top-level public sector leader does not work as hard as possible to compromise? Will the top-level public sector leader check out of conflict too soon and not do the work, heavy lifting, or deal-making necessary because their legacy has already been made? Inevitably, it is the remaining staff who are left feeling like they were used in a high-stakes game of chess or led into a battle that the leader was leaving with "all or nothing."

Summary Remarks

Reviewing the personal factors — beliefs, mindsets, and skills-- that top-level leaders bring to their positions demonstrates how they mix with the current context and current structural arrangements. These variables and mental filters can further complicate an already complex environment. None stand alone. The personal leadership characteristics of the top-level leader can be as powerful a structure as an actual physical structure. They are a way of thinking and an additional lens through which the individual leader understands their circumstances; consequently, these mental mechanisms influence their behaviors.

Anticipating the resistance many top-level leaders have shown on this topic, additional cautions are in order. If early in a new administration, the top-level leader adopts a leadership style that is quick and responsive while prioritizing the needs of the elected officials, if not overdone, this serves to create a perception among elected officials that the top-level leader and their executive team are aware and sensitive to the political needs of the council or board. This can create an early sense of teamwork and trust. I must stress that this could only be successful if not overdone. Overdoing it looks like making a wish list commitment to the elected officials without consulting staff on timing or feasibility and thus incurring resistance from the very players who need to execute the plans. Or it looks like the top-level public sector leader assuming their newly appointed position with preconceived beliefs about what the executive team needs and lecturing staff on how he is going to change the culture of the organization.

A top-level leader's personal characteristics are not neutral. They can mix favorably, and sometimes not, with the current context and current structural arrangements.

Endnotes

[1] Citation source confidential.

[2] For more information on the concept of "the undisciplined pursuit of more," see *Why the Mighty Fall: And Why Some Companies Never Give In*, by J. Collins (2009), pp. 21, 45–64.

[3]

[4] Citation source confidential.

[5] Citation source confidential

[6] Citation source confidential.

[7] Noonan (2007).

Chapter Four

Blind Spots that Lead to Errors in Judgment

This chapter focuses on the types of blind spots that lead to errors in judgment and the problematic actions I see repeatedly committed by top-level public sector leaders. These blind spots occur frequently enough to warrant examination. I also list a few examples of elected officials whose blind spots ended their careers poorly and tarnished their reputations. These missteps were avoidable and even solvable in many cases. As an advocate of the public sector profession, my goal is to decrease the prevalence of the scenarios similar to those detailed in this chapter.

Top-level leaders will inevitably have blind spots. These are compounded with the complexity of the current context, current structural arrangements, and the leaders' own personal beliefs, mindsets, and skills. Although leaders may not see these blind spots, they impair judgment nonetheless. They may stem from a character issue internal to the individual or perhaps a complex situation that instigates a certain set of behaviors. The behavior could be the result of an event, a person, a situation, or debilitating self-talk learned over time that then triggered the leader.[1] It is not unusual during my consultations to discover, with the consultee, a blind spot that has its roots in early childhood and family life.

What follows is a discussion of the blind spots I observed throughout my research. It is hard to overstate how frequently a misstep or scandal is made worse by an ethical blind spot. While the current context, current structural arrangements, and the leader's personal characteristics are certainly enough to create difficult situations to trip up even the most experienced public leader, what is likely underlying a misstep or scandal is an ethical blind spot. Many of these blind spots have also been discussed in the larger field of business ethics research[2] and in the work of Bazerman and Tenbrunsel,[3] which have greatly influenced how I categorize and explain the blind spots I observed.

Hubris—Public Sector Style

Hubris exists when a leader or manager becomes overly self-confident or arrogant. They see success as virtually guaranteed or as something they're entitled to, given their past successes. Or, they believe that they have a firm grasp of the situations they are facing and can outsmart any opposition.

Collins[4] called this "hubris born of success." He argued that the rhetoric of success, "We're successful because we do these things well," replaces a penetrating understanding and insight; that is, "We're successful because *we understand why* we do specific things well and under *what conditions they would no longer work*." Organizational players can lose sight of the true underlying factors that created success in the first place.

In the public sector, this can take the form of a "Joan of Arc" kind of hubris, where the leader stays in the complex situation or exerts their leadership into any and all situations because they believe they alone can solve the intractable problem. "Joan of Arc" was first used by a public sector leader who, in fact, admittedly suffered from this form of hubris. Innumerable top-level public sector leaders will elect to stay in a clearly bad environment to save their staff or shield them from the political environment or because they feel they have the political influence to survive the misstep and/or to dramatically change the dynamics, only to become a casualty in that increasingly complex political environment they felt they knew so well. The hubristic belief that their years of experience or their past relationships with relevant players will ensure that they can successfully navigate a highly public scandal or misstep has led to the premature departure of too many.

Luck, timing, a full "bank account" (i.e., IOUs accumulated from having successfully delivered in the past) with elected officials that allows a certain degree of freedom, the support of talented staff, and an ample budget all play a role in many leaders' successful outcomes in the public sector. Those who fail to acknowledge the role played by these factors tend to overestimate their own merits and capabilities. For example, perhaps a top-level public sector leader is dealing with a budget windfall or a tragedy in the community, and the staff comes through beautifully. Perhaps a major capital project was on the books during a leader's tenure, and it was popular and well-funded. Taking credit for successes like these, believing that they were the direct result of a leader's skills alone, losing sight of the help provided by others, and walking and talking with an overconfidence that can be fun to be around but borders on arrogance is dangerous. This leads to cockiness and, consequently, a tendency to make quick, bad decisions that require backtracking later or rationalizations so extreme that those involved reframe their actions as though they weren't even there when the decision was made in the first place. If this overconfidence somehow does not get the top-level public sector leader in trouble the first few times because many leaders are equally quick to repair the damage, the lack of consequences reinforces the idea that it is not their thinking that is problematic but the execution. Hubris, in action, puts a wall up around the leader, creating a false sense of invincibility.

The belief that one will continue to be successful almost automatically is hubris. And the belief that the individual leader themselves is especially talented, clever, and skilled and that this was the reason for their previous successes, again, creates an overconfidence that, when overexpressed, is perceived as arrogance. Arrogance is sneaky; it flows and ebbs each day, appearing most often when the stakes are particularly high or, deadlines are near or when the political environment requires a direction or decision. The ambiguity or stress resulting from the raised stakes leads the leader to demonstrate the riskiest behaviors to reinforce the basis of their hubris rather than the most cautious behaviors, which might reveal that, like most, they don't know or control everything.

This false sense of invincibility[5] is best demonstrated by the 1986 NASA Challenger tragedy and the subsequent research conducted to understand the group dynamics involved in that decision to launch. The management team, and to some extent, the Engineering team, had believed that their past successes, specifically the 19 past successful launches, would ensure their future success. This assumption by management and not necessarily the engineers, among other dynamics, influenced the launch/no-launch decision. Invincibility in the public arena is a dangerous assumption and a crushing blind spot. The notion informing this sense of invincibility is that past correct decisions inevitably lead to future correct decisions—because *you* made the decision, so it must be right. The danger of this is obvious. It leads to uncritical acceptance, groupthink on a team, and potentially bad decision-making and recommendations that lead to bad public policy. During public sector leadership presentations, Craig Dunn, PhD, the helpful colleague who collaborated with me on early discussions about public sector ethical dilemmas, cautions public sector leaders: "Never underestimate your ability for self-deception."

This first blind spot is the most difficult to change and address when, for example, coaching a top-level public sector leader, much less a mayor, city council member, board chair, or legislative elected official. Those who occupy these roles thrive on their expertise, connections, and the confidence that comes from having been in the field. Their years of experience in these positions are also often the source of their confidence; subsequently, this very confidence is often a source of their influence. It is not uncommon to hear the following from the leader, "I have seen this happen many times before." Yet, in fact, they fail to see that these situations have not happened *this way* many times before because the players have changed; the city councils, county boards, or water agency communities are different now. Over time, these stakeholders have developed different values and goals than those of past groups. Often, the leaders' overconfidence causes them to fail to see that circumstances have changed enough that the typical fix will not work.

Hubris has a negative, amplifying cycle. If a person is arrogant, they take any critique as questionable; the questioning of the critique and the subsequent response reinforces their confidence and arrogance, which creates more arrogance and self-certainty. A coach or a staff member who attempts to ask penetrating and reflective questions of a leader who acts with hubris runs the risk of being labeled as a naysayer or not a team player. Those who aren't perceived as team players in the public arena are iced out. Once iced out, these unfortunate members of the community have no timely information or influence, no context to speak up within, and, hence, no power.

Typically, if a leader acts with hubris, most of the time, staff will not even venture into the arena of questioning decisions or actions. They know the label this will leave them with. So, they join in, play their role in implementing plans, and when it all goes south, remark that they knew this would happen. One is left to ask, "Why didn't you say something in the first place?" and the cycle simply repeats itself because saying something, risking the "not a team player" label, is too high a price in the public arena. Bazerman recently published a book called *Complicit* (2022), in which he studied in great detail how coworkers, professional colleagues, friends, and family members often stand by, observe, and enable unethical behavior. This is worth reading if you want to understand how the structures informing our context can drive or at least encourage unethical behavior and, in the cases discussed here, missteps and misjudgments.[6]

A related idea worth examining further is that a confident top-level public sector leader is fun to be around. Their swagger can be energizing, and the exciting environment they create reinforces their and team members' behaviors. Over time, an in-group or team blind spot is created, one that is in everyone's interests to ignore; the team is along for the ride and the successes that come. This swagger and team euphoria is nearly impossible to penetrate unless one can show specifically, with a scenario that brings fear to the leader, how it is hurting their best interests, credibility, or legacy. Usually, it takes a colleague with more years of experience or greater stature than the leader to intervene, and interestingly, those senior players are almost never willing to. This is especially the case for elected officials; they tend not to coach or give each other advice or warnings. They worry about having their motivations questioned. Few interventions short of a scandal could end the amplifying cycle of this type of hubris.

Another form that hubris takes is that of "the rules don't apply to me." While this is not often a conscious or even stated belief, it is acted upon in practice: "I don't have to act with caution, but I expect you to act with caution as staff. I don't have to be thorough in my analysis, but I expect you to do a complete analysis as staff." The notion is that the leader is on a higher plane where intuition and relationships are primary and exchange is understood. Furthermore, the leader can take risks that anyone below them cannot. Lower-level staff do not act with the same hubris as higher-level leaders. This makes sense, given the roles, responsibilities, and burdens the top-level public sector leader is paid to shoulder. As a result, this arrogance develops with the time, experience, success, and power that comes with outlasting the elected officials who come and go every four to eight years.

It is worth noting that, unlike the private sector, a hubristic public sector leadership style does not typically involve any of the financial perks that might come with hubris in the private sector, such as frequent bonuses, an extremely high salary, extravagant spending on entertainment, lunches, conference trips to glamorous locations, elaborate office furnishings, or expensive company cars. The currency in the public arena is influence, getting projects passed and implemented, solving problems and improving services for citizens, improving the work environment for employees, making life for citizens easier and better, gaining favorable headlines/stories in print or social media, and achieving successes by delivering on the promises of elected officials. This is hubris in service of others, which makes it harder to challenge and to see as problematic on both the parts of the individual leader involved and those around this leader.

One additional note: public organizations are seriously impacted when a leader acts with hubris during their departure. I observed a few top-level public sector leaders in agencies, cities, and counties across the State of California who no longer enjoyed the support of their boards or councils. They pushed back against the critique, refused to resign or retire, battled their boards, and engaged in behind-the-scenes pressure to overturn the desires of the board or council to replace them. They ended their careers without grace and left staff unsettled by the turmoil. The ensuing decision regarding their replacement was influenced by the chaos of their departure and, for years, affected the morale of the organization and the dynamics of the boards and councils.[7]

Moral Hypocrisy/Double Standards

Case example:

A top-level public leader in the field of law enforcement was found to have utilized her office stationery to write a letter of recommendation for college admission as a favor for a select political supporter—an action she had expressly forbidden other staff from engaging in. A few years later, she decided to retire, and this misstep, along with a couple of other misjudgments, put a stain on an outstanding career.

Moral hypocrisy occurs when one's understanding and evaluation of one's own moral transgressions differ substantially from their evaluations of the same transgressions committed by others. This is another version of the "rules don't apply to me" mentality.

There are public officials at the elected official level and the top public sector leader level who engage in behaviors that they criticize others for or have set outright prohibitions against in their organizational norms and values, and administrative code. For example, a big city elected official was accused of sexually harassing and verbally abusing his own staff while he held himself up as a progressive politician on social issues. After offering an apology to citizens and resigning from office, he later pleaded guilty to one felony and two misdemeanor charges. He is not alone in this "the rules don't apply to me" behavior. A high-profile state's elected official found himself in this situation in 2021 and resigned from his office after an investigation he ordered. A top-level public leader in academia working for a state university in a populous state lavishly spent money on travel expenses when there were policies that he was responsible for enforcing system-wide to prohibit such behavior. A top-level leader in the United States Navy violated the Navy's prohibitions against pornography on government laptops while lecturing the troops about following the rules. Over the past two years, a continuous list of leaders in the United States Navy has made the news. This list has detailed those who accepted bribes, overt and covert, to direct business toward one particular vendor, leading to a system-wide scandal in a culture that is clear about the rules. A big city non-profit leader funneled money into her own personal bank account while fundraising for that same nonprofit and claiming a shortage of funds. A big city port agency's top-level leader, fully aware of conflict-of-interest rules for the agency, ran a side business that secured a port contract while also serving as a decision-maker in the selection process. A big state elected official sworn to uphold the state's constitution pleaded guilty to running a money laundering scheme, public corruption, gun trafficking, and bribery, all while in office. A top-level small city public leader who, over two decades, had earned the confidence and support of his mayor and city councilors, had violated his own rule about mixing the personal and the professional and engaged in an affair with a top-level subordinate.[8] Although this issue was not subject to investigation or a complaint from the subordinate involved, rumors floated through the organization for months. This did not earn him an early departure but robbed him of his credibility in the eyes of the staff at the end of his career.

At the time of writing, a top-level elected official in a big county jurisdiction just ended a promising bid for a higher state office due to an "improper" relationship that became contentious and public. Sex-related scandals are certainly not an uncommon occurrence and only scratches the surface of the number of examples I could mention in this category. However, it is a perplexing one because it does suggest a double standard in behavior and a genuine blind spot for leaders, who want to act on their attraction, which can lead to serious consequences for: 1) the organization in terms of the slow erosion of the credibility of HR policies when they are not equally applied; and 2) the involved players, their careers, family life, reputations, and future.

When these affairs and/or unwanted sexual behaviors hit the news, they create an internal and external lack of trust in government officials, which lasts long after the offending parties are gone. This blind spot is particularly disturbing and disruptive for leaders in positions of power; it causes them to act in ways that are flirtatious or overly familiar with lower-level staff without having the objective ability to see these behaviors for what they are. The gratification of the ego as a result of this behavior blinds leaders to its inappropriateness in a work environment.

Furthermore, this is an enormously dangerous blind spot once it takes hold and a difficult one to tackle. For example, who is going to tell the top leader to end the behavior if no one complains? Typically, offended employees fear they might lose their jobs if they do complain or if there is a relationship that appears to be consensual; no one noticing this wants to be the one to report it. Reporting it requires going above the top-level leader to the elected body or around them to Human Resources. It is my experience that direct feedback does not move the needle on this, as rationalizations are abundant. Additionally, what happens when there is a complaint, and it comes late after it turns out the offended employee has left and filed a complaint through a regulatory body? The ability of the offending party to self-manage and step outside oneself and imagine how they might be perceived at all times is what is required to catch this particular double-standard blind spot, which is also hubris. News stories that are repeated weekly and monthly about the downfall of leaders who behave in this way do not seem to do the trick. However, the following questions remain: How do you spot double standards when you act with hubris? How could you even see it?

Take, for example, the behavior of a medium-sized city top-level law enforcement leader who was frequently the face of the department. Whatever trigger set him off, he began berating staff selectively, wielding his power, and creating an intimidating environment, irrespective of how it went against the expressed wishes of his boss and his own expressed beliefs about how supervisors below him should behave. Complaints simmered and mounted for months and months. He was given feedback, coaching, and a chance to hear others' perceptions and the basis for them. This only increased his fury. He ultimately had a blowout, "no going back," verbal exchange with his boss and others. Soon after, he retired. The departure was cool, the celebration was muted, and his years of stellar service were overshadowed by these events.[9] A particular pain point here was how unnecessary this graceless departure was. He had earned ample respect and loyalty throughout his years of service and had such presence. However, he ultimately could not navigate or accept the growing perceptions that his hubris, moral hypocrisy, and the double standard between his behavior and his professed values had blinded him to the legitimacy of the feedback/critique. It is my conclusion that the circumstances of his career and the personal leadership characteristics, like beliefs, mindsets, and skills, outlined in Chapter Three haunted him and were unresolved.

I focus on this example not to belabor a blind spot or a specific case but to point out the necessity in the field of public sector leadership to step back, see how others might perceive us in our most successful moments, and check behaviors around potential blind spots. Here, I offer you the following advice: Ask others. Accept that there might be flaws in your performance and resolve past triggers and/or, if you prefer not to dive deep into yourself, devote serious and conscious effort to finding a way to take stock of how to enhance your self-management abilities.

This is a lesson I learned myself the hard way during the height of my busy career running the OEP. My proximity to the city manager, resulting influence, single-minded drive to quickly advance diversity efforts, and do battle with those who stood in the way, as well as my belief in celebrations and institutional events, got me called up short a few times. I had to stop and listen closely and realize what it felt like to be on the receiving end of my actions. Furthermore, I had to examine why my approach did not leave room for other tactics, take time to understand the human side of change, and how my actions might be creating a new kind of one-up/one-down dynamic. Luckily, a colleague was willing to confront me, and the leaders whom I had delivered for were willing to give me the benefit of the doubt and the space to change. I changed on a dime. As crushing and painful as those moments were, it was evidence to me that anyone can bounce back from a misstep depending on the context and what type of misstep it is. The more important lesson I learned was that these experiences create more awareness of one's blind spots in the future.

Less dramatic or subtler forms of moral hypocrisy by top-level leaders or managers have been perpetrated by leaders who demand loyalty and good character from their staff and often discipline them if they don't demonstrate this. Furthermore, elected officials themselves get caught operating with a different set of rules because elected officials operate with a different moral code. The elected moral code is a political one, not an administrative one. The political code is, "What do I need to do to get reelected? What do my constituents need, and how can I get that for them?" This is not an illegal code; it is just a different one. Elected officials have a constituency they are serving—those who elected them. When an elected official suddenly changes course, it is likely that their constituents have expressed dissatisfaction with their work. Top-level public sector leaders implement the policies these elected officials dictate, so the arenas have different functions; one is political, and the other is administrative and operational. Top-level public sector leaders straddle these worlds. It is an infrequent occurrence, for example, when a city or county top-level leader steps outside the administrative code and acts overtly politically on behalf of and in service of the elected official. However, when this happens, it is almost always the city manager or county administrator who takes the fall, not the elected official.

As a lecturer for upper-division ethics classes, every semester, I inevitably deal with a handful of students who want me to adjust their grades and raise their final score a point higher, even after I had already bumped their grades if the final number ended in .5 or higher as well as added a class curve. They want an extra bump despite this because they "really want" (or "need") a B rather than a B-. When I point out that it's simply not fair to just do it for them—what if all the dozens of other students want this same favor, too?—they do not see this as a contradiction because the others don't need it as much as they do or they don't need to know I made this exception. Nor do they see a contradiction in certain types of cheating because they believe the system is selectively difficult for them to navigate, they work harder than everyone else, and if they cheat, this is okay because books cost too much and the system is unfair and overly bureaucratic. The rationalizations are numerous.

The double standard is that they don't think the rules apply to them, but they think that others should follow the rules. Ergo, the city manager who expects loyalty and good character but does not demonstrate this same good character in managing up to elected officials, is a prime example of someone who embraces the double standard. This is a psychological process of rationalizing and compartmentalizing. A form of elitism or exceptionalism exists when our own vested interests (professional, personal, social, or economic) blind us to our own inconsistencies. In research on white-collar crime, Soltes[10] discovered that the subjects he interviewed had an amazing ability to rationalize. They understood intellectually that they had hurt people, but the harm they perpetrated did not resonate emotionally. For them, it was not criminal because no one was killed. The white-collar criminal tends to view their deeds not as a deception but rather as pragmatic behavior; they comfortably engage in "I wanted the money, so I took it" sort of thinking. Soltes suggested that we are all quite capable of rationalization and compartmentalization. This is what the field of ethics calls cognitive barriers in ethical awareness.[11]

Ethical Fading

In the face of great uncertainty and tough ethical dilemmas about what to do in a particular situation, there can be a narrowing of one's focus. For example, phrases like "Let's just make a business decision here," "We have to find a way to please the mayor on this," "Put your management hat on now," "It's time to make an engineering decision and make this less complicated; stop worrying about the community," or "Let's make this decision now, and we can deal with the rest later" exemplify the contexts in which ethical fading can occur. The seriousness of the ethical dilemma fades as solutions and decisions become too difficult to implement. Leaders and staff alike might elect to cut corners to avoid the most troublesome parts of the solution. Thus, the focus narrows to what can be solved. The bar for a true solution may be lowered. Instead, they might settle for a strategy that solves only a part of the issue. Thus, the larger ethical dilemma that requires a solution becomes obfuscated in the process. This is especially poignant when the top-level public sector leader cannot influence or convince elected officials of a viable solution to ethical dilemmas. The administrative staff are then forced to settle for something they can live with. There is comfort in achieving the more narrowed action, and this becomes part of the rationale for the action, which consequently leads to ethical fading. Bazerman and Tenbrunsel argued that "everyday work life—including goals, rewards, compliance systems, and informal pressures—can contribute to ethical fading, a process by which ethical dimensions are eliminated from a decision."[12]

The blind spot forms around how to solve the ethical dilemma, whether it is deciding what to do about toxins in the Flint, Michigan water sources, failures in the Mississippi drinking water crisis, toxic materials in railroad box cars that may be unsafe upon impact, when and if to inform the public, whether to insist that employees cannot be moved into a building that is not ready to be safely occupied, or whether narrowing one's focus requires the team to dismiss the concerns of a presumed "naysayer" engineer about the O-ring issue. How to do away with the uncertainty or anxiety that a dilemma presents and how to solve a serious problem (such as homelessness, gun laws, asbestos containment in a city-owned building, or contaminated drinking water) without doing the work to really solve it are the focuses of ethical fading.

Any misstep can fall into several of these blind spot categories, and while the categorization of a misstep is not always required, it is helpful to see where the propensity for a misstep lies in the public arena or in a particular organization or profession. If those of us in the public arena know where the likely missteps will happen, we may want to implement a mechanism to ensure it does not happen. For example, the Mr. Charisma case study might have been an example of ethical fading. Perhaps the big city RTC leader's misstep was he wanted to deliver on a much-desired project and/or contribute to the legacy of the chair of his board, or simplify the complexity of the issue on the ballot statement for citizens, and narrowed his focus. He relied on a trusted insider versus the contrarian voices of other members of his staff, and that might have been the ethical fading blind spot. Hubris certainly played a part, but ethical fading, given its particular prevalence when one narrows their focus, might be more frequent among planners, engineering staff, and transportation experts who face complex choices or dilemmas that do not have clear, clean answers. Treating a dilemma in a technical, focused manner, setting aside the larger implications, could be a serious temptation. I caution professionals in these professions to keep this pitfall in mind and develop and institute mechanisms to forestall a misstep. (see Chapter Six for more elaboration on mechanisms).

The "Want to Win" Takes Over

Bazerman and Tenbrunsel referenced a study in which women students interviewing for positions were asked before the interview how they might answer inappropriate questions from the interviewer. For example, they were asked how they might respond to questions such as, "Do you have a boyfriend?" "Do people find you desirable?" or "Do you think it is necessary for women to wear bras to work?" In all cases, these young women predicted that they would refuse to answer the questions, ask why these questions were being asked, and/or walk out of the interview.

In fact, when these questions were asked, none of the interviewees refused to answer them. A few did ask why the questions were asked, but they did so politely at the end of the interview. Note that this study took place in the early 2000s before the #MeToo movement took the country and culture by storm in 2018. The responses might certainly be different now. Yet, the authors' broader conclusion is worthy of attention: We tend to predict that we will be more ethical than we will actually be. In many cases, the want to "win"—the interview, the prize we are seeking—takes over. We have a tendency to want to walk away with something as a result of our efforts, and this desire to win blinds us to what is ethical.[13]

This idea can apply to the behaviors of public sector leaders who want to win the argument, best the council member or mayor, or beat out the competing jurisdiction, and this leads to behaviors that impact careers. The importance of the EQ concept of self-management comes into play here.[14] The necessity to self-manage one's behavior and resist the urge to use the considerable power the top-level public sector leader has at their disposal to put the competition in their place is considerable.

As previously mentioned, while some of these blind spots and/or cognitive limitations overlap, it is important to call them out because they are precursors to later over-the-top hubristic behaviors. There are many top-level public sector leaders who are experienced or have successes under their belts and can leave an argument or observation they have alone or save it for another day. Then there are those who "can't help themselves" in their desire to "win the day" by reminding people who is in charge, and it is these leaders who show concerning traits that will get them in trouble later.

For example, there are top-level public sector leaders who regularly create leadership style missteps in that they control and cut off their staff during public presentations with elected board members or write the script, not just review the script for any staff presentations to control what is said. They might even go as far as attempting to control the direct daily interactions between their elected officials and staff, external consultants, and citizens.[15]

There is a price to be paid for this sort of controlling leadership. While they may believe they have successfully managed perceptions, they have forgotten that those controlling interventions, day after day, year after year, create within the staff not only passivity and complacency but also resentment and a built-up need for revenge in subliminal ways. It is precisely this dynamic—where staff stand on the sidelines and do not warn the leader when they see political trouble brewing because they are simply fed up. Their loyalty has long dissipated, and the leader's demeaning behavior has taken its toll—that is dangerous to the leader. These leadership behavior-missteps inescapably result in class action complaints that bypass the institution and go straight to the press, as well as surprisingly wicked sabotage from within the organization that is leaked to outside stakeholders and institutions. This decimates the reputations of individuals and their institutions.

On a completely different and perhaps surprising note, humor or playfulness generally considered acceptable can quickly be perceived as an error in judgment or a questionable character issue when this playfulness is overexpressed, all because the leader wanted "more" approval or attention. An example of this is a top-level public sector leader of a small city who perhaps wanted to win the support and affection of local union leadership after difficult negotiations. Alongside another top-level public safety leader, they put on an inappropriate skit to become "one of the boys" or perhaps to "win them over with humor." This resulted in an outcry from a number of public safety and general employees and from community members who watched city hall closely. Even after issuing an apology and admission of poor judgment, it was a hard misstep to comprehend and accept. In another case, the competitive instincts of a top-level public sector leader allowed her to best her well-respected competition to get the job, but she could not leave it at that and had to also denigrate and bad mouth this respected leader. Thus, she lost the support of the staff because of the character issues this highlighted.

Another top-level public sector leader challenged a board member at a public reception event regarding her allegiances to prove that he was right all along about his beliefs regarding the veracity of the ethical conduct of the agency she often touted and supported. He made his point but lost the confidence of many of his board members in the process because of the public nature of his confrontation and the fact this same behavior had been demonstrated previously.[16] The view of public sector leaders who do not "let go" of their perceptions of other agency leaders, even when they are correct perceptions, is a tricky issue for board members or elected officials. They expect the person who represents their agency to "get over it" or be the bigger person and not take past actions, outrageous or not, personally. This is a tall order, rarely one these board members adopt for themselves, but they do expect it of the leaders that run their agencies and take note amongst themselves when enough is enough. This is a lesson for any top-level public sector leader to learn. I have watched with worry during vulnerable moments of conference or workshop receptions where alcohol is served, or the lunchtime conversation turns more candid and personal, and the top-level public sector leader does not have their self-management skills on high alert and becomes too informal and chatty, and the drive to win the point is made. Board members and elected officials watch, too, and conclusions are drawn.

These actions are not all hubristic per se, and they do not necessarily constitute a moral hypocrisy/double standard; however, these are different sorts of blind spots that are worthy of attention. The "want" that can take over requires some self-reflection on the part of top-level public sector leaders who know they can get especially competitive. While interviewing elected officials on their pet peeves about city or county staff, I discovered that one of the most frequently mentioned sore spots for elected officials regarding their city and/or county managers specifically is when they see them try to one-up or "win the argument" with an elected official, say the last "winning" point at a board meeting, or best the council member's humor with more "winning" humor or cleverness.[17]

Ethical Spinning

The concept of ethical spinning, as it applies to the behaviors of top-level public sector leaders, is the rationalizing of questionable behavior over time, which changes what is regarded as ethical behavior in the organization. The thought processes involved are slippery slopes. What is ethical undergoes continuous redefinition based on past unethical behaviors that were accepted. Staff become desensitized to what is considered appropriate or acceptable.

Consider some of the following phrases heard in the halls of public organizations:

- "Whatever it takes…."

- "Do we need to make that public?"

- "Should I tell them everything I know or wait for them to ask?"

- "It is the only way to get this through the board."

- "They don't need to know the details, so just do what you need to do to get it passed."

- "We can deal with the specifics later...."

Of course, the frequency of comments like these depends on the leadership and tone at the elected level, as well as the tone of the top-level leadership style.

In 2007, a top-level public sector leader of a medium-sized water district, when asked by a regulating body why their agency had overstated the revenue financing required for the sake of passing a $77 million bond issue, joked that it was "a little Enron accounting." In the big city RTA example, the investigative report suggested that a number of top-level leaders had ignored staff pleas for transparency about a project's cost projections that were too rosy and suggested that the agency was misleading the public and decision-makers about the true costs. Given that no one was making personal gains on this, and the project was laudable, and in the interests of the region, it is my analysis that this was not seen as an ethics issue by the staff. It was an issue of accuracy about the projections or staff rivalry about whose competing analysis won favor with higher-ups. This is a form of ethical spinning and ethical fading. In the big city Real Estate Deal previously discussed, it could be argued that the staff put themselves into the building, or they were directed to do so before it was ready to save the mayor the embarrassment of the cost per day of keeping it vacant. However, this ethical spinning led to numerous consequences, such as potential health concerns regarding the transferred staff's exposure to asbestos, a class action lawsuit, and the dismissal and/or resignation of staff members who approved the transfer.

There is another kind of ethical spinning that is not clear-cut because it only surfaces because norms about what should be transparent have changed over time. This is especially dangerous as expectations and accountability change and oftentimes the workforce's behaviors don't change in kind. Two examples of this come to mind. In both cases, the top-level public sector leaders did not see that times had changed and that the political body no longer accepted certain behaviors or attitudes from staff. The staff ignored the citizens or other city/county departments one time too often. Ultimately, everything blew up. In the first example, one big public mistake in how the billing rates were calculated by staff in a big city's operations department that affected many customers led to the top-level replacement of staff. It appeared to be less about the mistake, which was undoubtedly indefensible, but this issue was heightened by the big city department leadership's defensive reaction to the critique. The elected officials did not want to hear an explanation as much as they wanted a thorough apology, acknowledgement of the mishandling of the calculation, and perhaps a resignation. The second case shows how a backlog of unaddressed cases overseen by a big city's public safety department can end a career if the right corrective actions are not taken and/or the situation is not deftly handled. Again, in this case, the observed reason the situation was not successfully handled was the defensive reaction from the section head leader, who held onto a righteous belief in the "here's what we were thinking" rationale. They ultimately defended their "here is all that we are really required to do" rationale as if that were sufficient to address the mistake. Neither political leaders nor the public wanted to hear such explanations in this environment where trust in the government was low. The beliefs and attitudes of the political body and the community had changed, and those involved in the missteps had missed this. This is a very tricky and subtle sort of dependence on ethical spinning that did not work.

These examples suggest that the slow deterioration of what is considered ethical can easily go unnoticed. In the public sector, there are frequently ethical dilemmas when leaders are faced with major infrastructure projects and the deadlines, costs, and political capital required to complete them. It is so easy to rationalize marginally, if not blatantly, unethical behaviors to "just get the project done" to please the public, a community group, or an elected official or to meet a deadline so that the project costs do not skyrocket. How can one dispute the importance of keeping a project within the budget? This is a laudable goal. But what if doing so requires you to ignore a mandated open competitive process to hire a subcontractor, which can be more time-consuming? Committing an ethical fault to save time or money often makes doing this seem less problematic. It is important to restate that none of this involves personal financial gain or pay-for-play activities. The motivation is always to complete the project on time, within the budget, and with a high level of quality. At the same time, the "whatever it takes to get it done" scenario corrupts the organizational culture over time. As explained by Mr. Astute Engineer (referenced in later chapters): "The 'whatever it takes to get it done' is how the staffer is put in an untenable position. Be a naysayer, and your career is damaged or over, or follow through as ordered and take the fall when it doesn't work."[18] This is the classic double-bind no employee should be put in.

Let's revisit a former high-profile-state elected official's resignation to make another point about ethical spinning. As a result of his inappropriate behavior with several of the women in his office, he ordered an investigation to clarify the facts and prove his innocence. The investigators found that many of the women who worked for him had raised their discomfort with the sexual nature of his behavior with HR staff. These women were simply moved to another location in the former leader's office, coached to understand his intent versus his impact, and taught similar rationalizing actions. It appears that the staff, over time, lowered the bar on what was acceptable behavior due to many typical factors, such as the good work the top-level leader was doing regarding COVID, his family name, their loyalty, and their commitment to him.

These ethical dilemmas and choices spring up constantly in the public sector. They surface by way of HR issues but also when executing major infrastructure projects, specifically public–private collaborations. In these projects, the two sectors operate under different values, and what matters in a public arena, such as transparency, accuracy, budgeting, and accountability, is not always what matters to private sector contractors. It is inevitable that ethical dilemmas arise.

A Word About Revisionist History

The chart by Bazerman and Tenbrunsel[19] below outlines a dynamic that can occur when an ethical dilemma called a "revisionist history," or selective memory, occurs. This dynamic suggests that we remember behavior in a way that supports our self-image.

Perceptions of One's Own Ethicality
"Are You As Ethical As You Think You Are?"

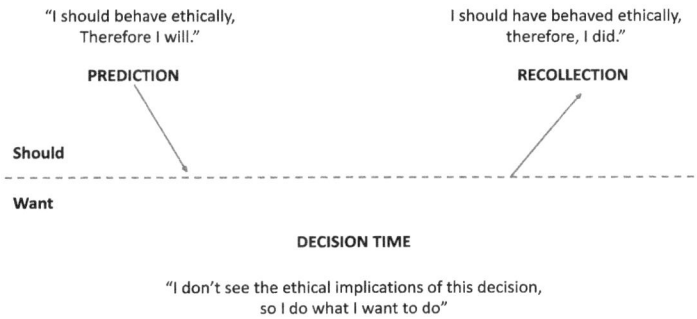

"I should behave ethically, Therefore I will."

I should have behaved ethically, therefore, I did."

PREDICTION

RECOLLECTION

Should

- -

Want

DECISION TIME

"I don't see the ethical implications of this decision, so I do what I want to do"

Taken from by Bazerman and Tenbrusel, Blind Spots: Why We Fail To Do What's Right and What To Do About It. 2013.

Similar to ethical spinning, the blind spot of the revisionist history fallacy is puzzlingly difficult to break through when coaching an offending party. They don't see the blind spot because they don't recall engaging in such a behavior and because they don't believe they could possibly engage in this behavior, given their imagined version of themselves. Even with evidence, such as quoting their words back to them, they believe they are above critique. Consider the following performance-related scenario, which demonstrates the seriousness of this blind spot. A high-level public sector leader believes she is justified in presenting her perspective and behavior as the right approach and can't see that her perspective is not what her boss wants to be presented to the staff or the community. Because she can't imagine that she would do anything that would hurt her boss, especially because she knows best what her boss needs, she can't accept any critique or feedback about her behavior.[20] This is a serious matter for both the staff below this leader and the bosses above.

Summary Remarks

In concluding this chapter on blind spots, I reiterate that it is not one variable that contributes to the creation of detrimental blind spots but **the interplay** between the blind spots a leader may possess and the variables in the current context and current structural arrangements (Chapter Two), as well as the leader's personal beliefs, mindsets, and skills (Chapter Three), that are at the **apex of the problem.** Systems thinking[21] is helpful here. The systems thinking approach suggests that one factor cannot by itself explain a problematic situation; instead, all factors surrounding the problematic action must be dissected. That is, by taking a system's thinking approach to the issue of careers that end badly, we can see that one variable impacts another, which creates another variable, and these connections can create negative loops that can amplify or drive a downward spiral or series of negative events. These are overlaying dynamics. One variable might trigger this downward spiral of career missteps, but multiple are usually required to continue the spiral. A misstep spawned by a complex current context plus the blind spot of hubris cause everyone to become tight-lipped because they don't know what to say, and even if they say something, they could be rebuffed. As a result, another blind spot of ethical spinning is created to explain the mistake, which leads to additional mistakes because people aren't sharing accurate information anymore and are basing their decisions on information that has been skewed. The cyclical nature of this reinforcing loop leads to another possible misstep by the leader.

Author Jim Collins said it succinctly in *How the Mighty Fall*: "I've concluded there are more ways to fall than to become great."[22] What Collins' quote offers to my argument here is that the complex environment in which top leaders work daily almost predicts a misstep unless navigated carefully. There are simply too many variables, complexities, and structures that can result in a misstep. The blind spots that leaders bring to the table in this complex environment create more opportunities for mistakes, missteps, and worse, scandals than success.

As you read this, do not make the mistake of nit-picking these particular situations or examples as those that have never happened and will never happen to you, your organization, or your executive team, thus absolving yourself. Many times, when this analysis was presented at conferences or during leadership academies, participants remarked, "Thank goodness, I am in the clear, as none of these things have happened to me." Or, they might say, "Thank goodness you aren't talking about me", or "This hasn't happened to me yet, so I guess I am doing fine." These statements are worrisome because they suggest a lack of caution and overconfidence, which can lead to at least one of the above blind spots.

It is rare for a top-level public sector leader not to have been confronted with ethical dilemmas that cause them to try to find a way out by considering ethical fading behaviors or ethical spinning to avoid blame. Or, they have adopted hubristic behaviors and believe that they are smarter than the problem because they have been successful to date with everything else. I have observed these behaviors in public organizations firsthand. While they are not illegal, and they are certainly human, I caution you to step back, think critically, and look at your relationships. Is your political capital with others low? Are there people waiting for you to make a mistake? Have you taken more than you've given to others, or are you perhaps not that easy to deal with? These are factors that should influence your decision about what next step to take. Furthermore, if you had the advantage of a council or board that supported you, but now a new election has changed the board composition and, consequently, the power dynamics, you are potentially at risk. These current structural arrangements variables might negatively impact you, and you must be aware of potential blind spots. Past successes may have led you to believe you'll continue to be successful, or a current mental model may be blinding you, but the fact remains that you can't see the new circumstances because you don't see the changed landscape and dynamics.

It would be fair for you to ask the following question: Do the variables outlined in the previous chapters always lead to a downfall or misstep serious enough to hurt one's career? The answer is no. There are numerous examples where one's likability or expertise has trumped the misstep, and the organization has looked the other way. This eats up one's political capital, but capital can be built back over time as long as there isn't another misstep. It is possible to make lemonade out of lemons if you acknowledge your mistake quickly, attribute the misstep to a learning curve, or perhaps fix the consequences of the misstep in a dramatic fashion, e.g., where there is a new beginning that benefits the organization. Reframe the mistake and address it and other problems, too—conducting a large redo, if you will—so that the original critique is eliminated and others take notice. This reframing can recast you as a leader not a victim of a misstep. Obviously, it depends on what the misstep was, how public it was, and the public leader's past history. The confounding factors are how serious the blind spots are and whether the current context or current structural arrangements are forgiving. Note that they are not typically forgiving, as these are highly political environments, but forgiveness is possible. The days of the "Teflon"[23] leader, where critique bounced off, are now scarce as the political environment has become more reported on, visible, and complex.

Given this discussion on how to recognize blind spots and deal with potential career missteps, it is important to pay attention to the **red flags** that signal a problem that might be coming or reveal a glaring ethical blind spot. Chapter Five outlines these **red flags** to help clarify what might be coming or what is already here, and Chapter Six details antidotes and mitigative actions that can be taken to deal with a future misstep, misjudgment, or scandal.

Endnotes

[1] "Trigger" or "trigger event" are terms used in the EQ literature to refer to the people, situations, words, or thoughts that cause a strong emotional reaction in ourselves. Our

reactions to our triggers are informed by our personal histories, including past experiences with a person or similar situation. It is important to know ourselves well enough to identify our triggers so we can "catch ourselves" and self-manage our behavioral responses to them. See *Emotional Intelligence 2.0* by Bradberry & Greaves (2009), pp. 16–17.

[2] Trevino & Nelson (2017).

[3] Bazerman & Tenbrunsel (2013)

[4] Collins (2009), p. 21.

[5] For a discussion about "invincibility" as a characteristic of the behavior that influenced the Challenger launch decision, see the previously referenced *Groupthink, Revised Edition,* by CRM Films (1998).

[6] Bazerman (2022).

[7] Citation source confidential.

[8] Citation source confidential.

[9] Citation source confidential.

[10] See *Why They Do it: Inside the Mind of the White Collar Criminal*, by Soltes (2016). See also Senturia's (2016) commentary in "White Collar Criminals Just Assume They Won't Get Caught."

[11] See Trevino & Nelson (2017), pp. 72–96. Chapter Three, "Deciding What's Right: A Psychological Approach," focuses on ethical awareness and the cognitive barriers that might get in the way of making good choices. One of the more frustrating discussions with the upper-division ethics classes I teach involve the rationalizations, a typical cognitive barrier, that students use to justify their behaviors. Even when confronted with the consequences of their choices, they still opt to favor "cheating" when they feel justified; not pay for required coursework books or required coursework software because they feel the prices are too high; accept favors from business owners who may be trying to manipulate them, believing that they can't be bought and deserve rewards for their hard work; generally do not see conflict-of-interest dilemmas at this point in their life experience; and see themselves as invincible to making a mistake and getting caught because they believe they will see the trouble coming. No matter how many examples I present to them of current, high-level, well-known business and public sector leaders getting in trouble due to their cognitive blind spots, they don't see this happening to themselves.

[12] Bazerman & Tenbrunsel (2013), pp. 30–31.

[13] Bazerman & Tenbrunsel (2013) added much to the "want versus should" and "want to win" research and psychological notion by taking it beyond just winning to wanting to walk away with something after all the effort. See Chapter Four, pp. 61–76, and Chapter Eight, pp. 152–156.

[14] See explanation of all emotional intelligence concepts (self-awareness, self-management, social awareness, and relationship awareness) in Bradberry & Greaves (2009). See also *The Emotional Intelligence Quick Book*, by Bradberry and Greaves (2015).

[15] Citation source confidential.

[16] Citation sources confidential for these examples.

[17] In 2007, in preparation for the Leadership and Management Academy presentations on "Power and Politics," and specifically the topic "How Elected Officials Think," I interviewed several local elected officials and asked them to share what they had observed about their city/county manager, department directors, or staff when they were on the receiving end of staff reports at the dais or in chambers. For example, I asked what non-verbal mannerisms they notice from staff that annoy them, irritate them, or cause them to lose trust. Are there ways that staff could present that would be more effective? How do they behave when the political winds change, and how should staff understand these changes in direction? Who do they ultimately serve? Who are their constituents, and what role should staff play? What do staff misunderstand about what matters most to them as elected officials? What frustrations, if any, do they have about how staff treat their constituents?

[18] Citation source confidential.

[19] For a discussion about this dynamic of revisionist history, see Bazerman & Tenbrunsel (2013), pp. 61–76.

[20] Citation source confidential.

[21] For an applied discussion about systems thinking and the relevance to the field of organizational dynamics, see the following resources: *The Fifth Discipline: The Art and Practice of Learning Organizations*, by Senge (1990); *The Fifth Discipline Field Book Strategies and Tools for Building a Learning Environment*, by Senge (1994) – systems thinking is addressed throughout the book but read closely the section "Systems Thinking" (pp. 87–190); "What is Systems Thinking? A Review of Selected Literature Plus Recommendations," by Monat & Gannon (2015); *Systems Thinking: Coping with 21st Century Problems*, by Broadman & Sauser (2008); *The Systems Thinking Approach to Strategic Planning and Management*, by Haines (2000).

[22] Collins (2009), p. 19.

[23] This term is used in the spirit of the *Urban Dictionary* definition of Teflon: "A person who seems to get away with EVERYTHING, no matter what it is! Nothing sticks to Teflon."

Chapter Five

Red Flags: Signals of Trouble Ahead

There are several ways through which an organization or individual members alert top-level public leaders of trouble that may be ahead. Warnings of trouble are typically subtle, and it takes a trusted right-hand person or executive staff member to draw the leaders' attention to these issues. The trusted staff member can also run interference and persistently address the warning signs in the best interests of the leader and the organization.

It is incumbent upon the leader to see the **red flags** themselves or to listen closely to others to avoid or quickly handle the very missteps this book discusses. This matters because how you handle your career matters; the steps you take impact your organization's reputation, staff morale, perceived confidence by elected officials in the leadership staff, and trust in the government by the community. The stability of power dynamics suffers consequences when elected officials, community groups, and staff lose faith and confidence in the leadership of the organization, and these consequences take years to rectify.

These **red flags** reflect the patterns I observed and documented, the research on ethical blind spots, the utilization of systems thinking, and a content analysis of the data and interviews conducted.[1]

The Language You and Others Use

Watch out for language like "just get it done" or "make it work." If you find yourself constantly having to justify an action, this is a **red flag**. If you hear others say, "This is a house of cards" or "I want to get out of this before everything falls apart," that's a **red flag**.

Watch for entitlement language like "We deserve this." This is a common statement that occurs just before a decision is made to hide data, cheat a competing agency, or settle a score.

Watch for when "what" you do becomes more important than "why" you do it. Collins (2009) found this to be a key mental model of organizations that have lost their purpose, a core rationale for their actions, and consequently, they fail.[2]

If you no longer hear statements like, "This is right," "This is wrong," "It is our duty to handle this and make it right," or "We must not ignore this any longer," this may mean the entire notion of serving the public has disappeared.

"I'm still having fun" could be a **red flag** because the situation has become about you, and your enjoyment of the ride has obfuscated the complexity and understanding of whether you are still effective. You might have a high threshold for chaos, complexity, and drama and, as a result, miss that something is amiss. Your job satisfaction is only part of the leadership equation. Your ability to continue to be credible and influential matters more than if the role is fun for you. "This isn't fun anymore" suggests that you see the difficulties and may not be able to address them. This may be a **red flag** that you feel burned out or have lost patience, and this might lead to quick or ill-advised decision-making. In either case, pay attention to what is behind these statements and dissect them carefully.

Staying For Really Cool Projects, Legacy Desires, or the Highest One-Year

Many top-level leaders in the public arena often stay too long, even in the face of tremendous hardships or unwinnable and complex scenarios, because they believe in a project and want to see it to completion. They support the staff and/or want to act as their buffer from political pressure. Furthermore, they might find the project challenging yet fulfilling and meeting an important community need, or perhaps they need the income to sustain their family, personal responsibilities, and obligations. Elected officials, in particular, want to be there for the ribbon cutting, and/or they want to do "one more project" or contribute to "one more policy decision" that solidifies their legacy or delivers on a political promise made during their campaign or by their board or city council. A decision by the public leader to stay longer than they wanted to stay is nearly always accompanied by the request of an elected official who needs that top-level leader to do the tough work and pave the way for them. However, they might not be there to back that same leader if the project gets controversial and goes south.

The most dangerous part of this **red flag** is the attractiveness of the "highest one-year" concept. Life-long public pensions are often based on the highest one year of pay (in some agencies, this is the highest three years), and this pay bump may have been made in a recent contract renewal. This can cause a leader to want to stay another year or more for several hundred dollars more a month during retirement. Given the complexities outlined in earlier chapters, the odds are higher that something bad is likely to occur in that one remaining year. Hubris and past successes usually create the false perception that leaders can outsmart any situation coming their way. They think they are the best person to handle these situations, and they are blinded by the competitiveness inherent in the desire to win a challenge (their "want" behavior), the increase in monthly pension payments, the project launch, or their legacy. Then boom—their reputations are soiled by a bad career ending.

My advice is to leave on a high note when possible. When leaders are excelling in the public eye, and their reputations are strong, they instinctively know, both logically and emotionally, that this is the hardest time to step away, as there is no clear reason to leave. However, this means that it is the right time to leave. I recommend leaving when you know that you have done a good job, everyone appreciates your work, you have given 100%, and the community and organization are better for it. You don't need to give more time in that role and risk your career ending badly. It is your own need for more, or your need not to disappoint others, that could ultimately result in a bad ending, and that is also harrowing for the organization.

Pressure to Take on Risky Projects Without Sufficient Data or Skills

Taking on risky projects when the data are ambiguous is a **red flag**. There is a tendency to put a positive spin on ambiguous data by amplifying the positive and not addressing or ignoring the negative. A former big-city top-level leader, Mr. Astute Engineer, said to me that he had seen city councils "emotionally make the 'go' decision"[3] before all the data were in. Staff do this, too. Then, they back into the rationale for the decision. The desire to please elected officials is a powerful driver here.

In police department debriefings about a shooting or an intervention, there is typically an analysis of how the event happened. What they often find is that highly infrequent situations (e.g., shootings) are high-risk environments, and if the officer lacks the skills needed to handle a shooting, they will almost surely contribute to a bad outcome. Organizations often do not face these sorts of unexpected situations; the situations an organization is ill-equipped to handle are often the ones that create the most significant and negative outcomes. While public sector staff cannot avoid these situations, it is a **red flag** for the top-level leader to be cavalier about how they are handled. Instead, they should be cautious. They must always remember that careers can easily be at stake. Public sector capital projects, real estate, and public/private partnerships require a constant state of alertness.

The message here is not to do nothing and take no risks but to have your eyes wide open at all times. Be careful not to underestimate the problems or assume you have the full picture, and tread carefully because this is your life's work, and it matters how you manage and end it.

Undisciplined Pursuit of More

Numerous private sector companies seek to expand their business beyond its original purpose or vision. Sometimes, these expansions work, and when they don't, it is usually because of the "undisciplined pursuit of more."[4] A subject previously mentioned in Chapter Three this involves pursuing more customers, more dominance in the field, more projects, and more of a brand when the passion, skills, or resources necessary for growth are not there to support this expansion. This type of expansion often violates the company's core values. This concept is a **red flag** for the public sector as well.

Public sector versions of this are pursuing public/private partnerships to solve a problem, but the public organization gets the short end of the deal. Or this could mean cutting a deal with a private developer to build a ballpark, but the partnership isn't equal because you are negotiating with public sector funds that often have limits, as creative financing is harder to pull off. Some leaders hire a big shot "known in the field," but these outsiders might not know the public sector, so they bring little to the problem that needs to be solved. As a consequence, they burn out quickly due to all the complexities. This could also mean dipping into pension funds or one-time money to solve an immediate financing problem and expecting the stock market to eventually make up the difference. Sometimes, leaders hire staff in large numbers to make up for past hiring freezes but use revenues that won't be there two years later.

Many creative financing options in the public sector can fall into the trap of the undisciplined pursuit of more, and it is not hard to see why. There is a window of increased revenues, and there is a specific moment in time to add staffing and resources to fund infrastructure projects or unmet needs that need to be addressed (e.g., filling potholes, buying office space, and hiring operations staff). This one-time money or blip in increased revenue might result in the rationale to "leave it to the next administration to figure out how to keep paying for the project in the future." The lack of discipline will ultimately involve the analysis of the impact several years down the road, and while a different administration might be conducting this analysis, these decisions have consequences for employees and citizens nonetheless. These decisions violate an unspoken value and norm about prudent risk-taking. Although the organization might not go bankrupt, like in the private sector, the city, county, or agency brand would still be damaged. Public confidence in the decision-making of public leadership erodes slowly when things go bad several years down the road with layoffs, legal suits, and unfulfilled promises.

One top-level public leader in a smaller city context described at length the history of his city negotiating bad deals with developers because elected officials wanted more projects to get the green light. When he came in as city manager, he instituted a philosophy that included a formula for ensuring that any project had to be a win for all three parties: the developer, the citizens, and the city organization. He wrestled back from the elected officials their involvement in the previous dynamic and changed the history of public/private partnerships in his city. He accomplished this soon after he had been hired, when he had their attention and greatest support. Understandably, this was a difficult dynamic to turn around.[5]

It is only fair to acknowledge that there is also a human proclivity on the part of the top-level public sector leader, not elected officials alone, to be undisciplined in their pursuit of more in a way that might violate a value that is unspoken. This could occur at any level, but the most consequential decision a public sector leader could make is pursuing a higher salary and negotiating a salary much higher than one's predecessor because they can or because the reputation of the organization is that it has a difficult community or difficult elected officials. This provides security and compensation for such an environment. Having greater benefits and perks than one's predecessor justifies the difficulties the position entails. This is completely understandable and absolutely smart at the personal level, and it actually creates an interesting power dynamic for the public sector leader with their elected official bosses initially. However, in one specific case, conclusions and impressions spread throughout the organization like wildfire because all information on compensation is public in the public sector. There is an unspoken value

88

or norm about "not being like the private sector." Thus, such negotiations may sit in the minds of staff, and the staff might make assumptions about future operations or policy decisions made by the leader as having been influenced by the comfortable package negotiated. And perhaps there might also be evidence to suggest that these deals sit uncomfortably with the elected body, who didn't appreciate the initial salary demands.

The big city RTA leader, Mr. Controversial Visionary, made very public salary demands. His salary requirements were significantly higher than those of his predecessor, so they were inevitably publicly challenged in a public board meeting by one of his board members. Eventually, it became a line in the sand for him. I do not suggest that he was not worthy of this demand, as he was recruited to make a turnaround in the organization. However, this demand was made in a context unfamiliar to the region, which placed him far above any of his contemporaries, and it seemed to violate the norm regarding what was "reasonable." Furthermore, it set very high expectations for him internally and externally. Perhaps this was not the undisciplined pursuit of more, but it felt like it then and still feels like it now, given the culture and norms the region was used to. I can't help but wonder if it became a thorn in the side of several board members, which made it even harder to find acceptance of his vision for the region.

Some have argued the DROP program[6] might fall in the bucket of "undisciplined pursuit of more." There are citizens who do not take kindly to this benefit, a benefit that had the intention to compensate public employees at the end of their careers for their lower incomes during their careers, compared to their private sector counterparts. Some citizens deeply resent this benefit, and it is unclear whether, at the time of voting on initiatives that could benefit the community's infrastructure, these same citizens voted against their very own interests for their communities due to this resentment.

The undisciplined pursuit of more can be a dynamic that informs policy, operations, projects, and even personal compensation packages.

Less Desire to Learn

A lack of inquisitiveness and the lack of desire to learn more about one's development as a leader is a **red flag** for any public sector leader. In one particular interview, the top-level public leader, Mr. Astute Engineer, who remained credible, influential, and out of the mix of any scandal throughout his entire 30-year-plus career, said he "never stopped thinking about how the dominos might fall."[7] If you are not thinking this way, this is a **red flag**. Another top-level leader, Mr. Wise and Noble Leader reflected on why he knew he was ready to retire: "After some time, you lose your edge...you get less interested in making government better."[8]

A dynamic I have observed and documented specifically with every city manager and county administrator who lasts longer than a year is that in their first one to three years, they tend to focus on getting the organization running and working well. They focus downward on the people who work for them. They care about the work environment, team development, relationship building with their staff and the community, and putting the right people in the right positions, and they work at being accessible to employees. After that three-year mark, there is a tendency to focus upward above them toward their bosses, the elected officials. Everything becomes more political as their confidence grows and elected officials figure out how to leverage that self-confidence. Relationships outside the organization also increase and develop into a network of connections. The leader is no longer focused on learning how to be a good leader internally but on how to achieve support externally, too. Both areas of focus matter, and both require the top-level public sector leader's attention if these leaders are to stay influential. If these focuses are not well balanced, this can lead to problematic operational issues, community issues, or political issues (this is what is referred to as the big "P" politics, that is, not the typical political dynamics within organizations but the political dynamics that involve elected officials and their interests).

Doing Battle with an Elected Official or Public Agency

If a leader is spending too much time fighting off a bad board member or a difficult public agency or they get the feeling that a few of their elected officials are getting impatient with them, bigger problems can occur if they get hooked or obsessed with winning or judgmental about the direction the agency is taking or the direction elected officials or board members are taking.

As previously mentioned in the Endnotes section for Chapter Four (see the section titled "The want to win takes over"), I conducted formal and informal interviews with several elected officials about what bothers them most about high-level staff when presenting to the council or the board of supervisors. The content from these interviews was part of my Leadership Academy presentation on how elected officials think. While this is not the place to share everything learned in those interviews, what they did reveal about a couple of the elected officials' pet peeves was enlightening and worth repeating. At the top of the list was "being interrupted" by an overzealous top-level leader or a top-level leader trying to be cleverer or funnier than the elected official. Or worse, if the elected official got the sense that the leader was trying to debate them and win the argument by having the last word, this left a particularly bad taste in their mouths. This is about trust, an unspoken protocol, and there are innumerable subtle ways that trust can erode between elected officials and their top-level public sector leaders. Rumors or gossip between political aides/administrative staff and operations staff, especially those who talk among themselves, manage to make their way back to the elected official and reduce trust, and you might never know these conversations happened. A big city top-level public sector leader once said to me that he would never talk badly about his bosses, city council members, and the mayor, as much as we wanted to hear his frustrations.[9] He had a sixth sense that this would infect his staff or him in ways that would show. It was a high bar and may have been an overly cautious approach that had the consequence of limiting his executive team's political EQ. Top-level staff often need to hear the top-level leader's thinking and what they are facing as they manage up. It can foster the development of the relationship, as you would trust your executive team with your frustrations and allow them to understand the strategies better by keeping them in the know. However, this leader erred on the side of keeping his experiences with the elected officials private to ensure his trustworthiness and avoid any possible perception that he was doing battle with them.

Losing Patience with Changes that Matter

A new city policy, a new city council or county board majority, or even one new council member or one new water board member can change the environment in a way that may be problematic for the top-level public sector leader. Yet, this is a fairly predictable dynamic, given the cycle of elections, so it is incumbent on the top-level leader to closely observe how this evolves with a keen eye for workability. Ask yourself: Are you losing patience as you onboard newly elected officials, and does it show? After one new board member was elected to a board that had not changed in decades, Mr. Wise and Noble Leader said, "I could see the handwriting on the wall...things were going to change."[10] It was not that the change was problematic per se; it was that, as more new board members were coming, there would be new norms, a new vision, potentially less camaraderie, relationship building from scratch, trust to build, and he wanted to close his career with the good feelings and reputation he currently had achieved. He did not need more to add to his sense of accomplishment. The structural arrangement of term limits had finally hit his jurisdiction and sparked him to assess his career and how he wanted to close it.

Over time, other changes in the current context or structural arrangements appeared for the other leaders I interviewed. Perhaps a prominent business or community leader who was a champion has left the region and is no longer there to go to bat for you. Or the media has become more difficult to influence and deal with and more demanding. They, too, have changed with the times, as their leadership changes or companies buy each other out or force out reporters and staff, and the demands of readers can mirror these changes. For example, X (previously Twitter), Instagram, TikTok, Facebook, blogs and online newsletters have created new media demands and dynamics. Mr. Wise and Noble Leader found this especially discouraging and said that the changes in the print and electronic media so frustrated him that it was a contributing factor to him leaving: "I left because…of the inability of the media to tell the story I told them about how good we are… taxpayers had no idea that governments were really good."[11] Essentially, he felt that the media was no longer interested in positive stories about the government. This was one factor that created an environment that was no longer acceptable to him.

Navigating new state or federal regulations that make operations or budgets impossible to manage is a way of life for public sector leaders, but if they were to have had years of experience handling these barriers and a new election suddenly brings more state or federal restrictions that they run out of patience, their irritation may begin to show. Staff will pick up on the message that their leader's heart isn't in it. It is easy to be flippant, irreverent, and sarcastic in this mental state; however, I urge you to be careful about this **red flag**, as a misstep is a likely outcome.

For example, a recent and not-so-subtle change occurred in the current context and current structural arrangements of a top-level public sector leader's role in a small Southern California city. This change in role had all the local and statewide top-level public sector leaders watching. The city council passed a new policy that removed the top-level leader's sole authority over the department head hiring process. The top-level leader subsequently "involuntarily" resigned his position because of this unilateral contractual change in his employment agreement. This was a dramatic change in the current structural arrangement of the city manager's roles and responsibilities. The top-level leader resigned the day this new administrative ruling was passed by the city council.

These examples are **red flags** for public sector leaders. If these changes create a persistent irritation that shows in your demeanor, if these changes create an environment where you cannot do your work to your level of satisfaction, or if they challenge your ethical bottom line, it is time to do some soul-searching about what you want/need before you make a misstep that challenges and compromises your reputation.

Externalizing Blame

Be careful about the messages you are giving your staff when something goes wrong. Are you using language that treats your circumstances like you are victims of the council, the board, the community, the new mandates, or another agency? This is dangerous territory in that it is a symptom of fatigue or that you have run out of creative solutions and ideas. Perhaps you are not willing or resent having to stretch to create new relationships, or you are not interested in learning a new, required technological skill. Perhaps too many intractable mandates or state-imposed structural changes have impacted your effectiveness and, thus, your vision, and you are exasperated and expressing this frustration outwardly toward those above you or outside the organization as responsible for doing this to you. These are all signs that it may be time to move on.

Erosion of Healthy Debate and Dialogue

The erosion of healthy debate/dialogue in the top-level public sector leader's executive team is a grave concern. This is often the *single biggest factor* leading to a leader's downfall. This occurs when management-level or high-level staff members begin refraining from telling a leader the truth, *not* due to a form of groupthink on the team but because the leader begins establishing a pattern of unreceptiveness. The staff member might have voiced their concerns or objections numerous times before, but they fell on deaf ears or were too quickly dismissed.

Or, there may have been a penalty for telling the leader the truth that made the leader uncomfortable. For example, they could have been on the receiving end of a cold shoulder, shut out of certain meetings or conversations, not copied on important emails, directed looks of irritation that many leaders silently use to say "enough" or "I don't approve of you bringing this up," interrupted repeatedly or not looked in the eye when speaking, repeatedly dismissed in a way that suggests they no longer have influence, or just quickly cut-off before they finish their point. Consequently, the staff members might feel they have no choice but to give up trying to advocate for another position or are increasingly intimidated or demoralized into silence. This can lead other team members individually, or even the executive team as a whole, to make mild suggestions if they think the leader is making a big mistake instead of *sounding the alarm loudly*. That is, they elect to let the leader walk off the cliff, even when they know there was a huge misstep ahead. As I write this paragraph, I can think of two executive teams in which this is happening right now. The staff are exasperated about how to influence a burned-out top-level leader in one case and incapable of getting the attention of the other leader who is a case study in hubris and lacking EQ.

Leaders need to set aside time to ask for debate and contrary opinions regarding the current course they are taking on a project, a budget item, a proposal, or a recommendation to the elected body. These contrary opinions should be sanctioned, encouraged, and rewarded. There should be no consequences for questioning the status quo. An easy way to do this is to build it into each meeting. This requires that the staff have the skills to advocate well for alternative options and ask good questions about the current course of action. Furthermore, this promotes the perception that there is experience in the room that the leader trusts.

One successful, longstanding, medium-sized city's top-level public sector leader said he realized his high-performing team was not telling him the truth about a project that was moving forward, and funds had already started to be used and the ribbon cutting had already happened. He asked one of his senior team members to challenge him at the next staff meeting to bring up the elephant in the room, which was him and his commitment to this project. This opened the door for others to chime in and speak the truth about what a bad project this was to continue, both financially and in terms of community support. Ultimately, the top-level leader took steps to bring the issue back to the city council, admit the mistake, and end the project.[12] This is a top-level public sector leader, a giant in his field, who had a high-performing team, and even he got it wrong. The team got into a rhythm of not challenging and questioning his decisions and each other, and they nearly missed the critical moment to backtrack on a poor recommendation they had made to the city council. If this can happen to a high-performing team that typically has healthy dialogue, this can happen to your team.

If a team does not engage in debate, fact-based dialogue begins to disappear, leading to poor decisions and performance. This ultimately leads to problems, scandals, or dismissals. *In every single case of a career ending poorly, there were executive- and lower-level staff who watched the disintegration happen.* Either they did not effectively step in, or they tried and were rebuffed. The common refrain is, "I saw this coming." If they did, why didn't they say so in a way that could be heard? Why didn't the leader hear them and correct their course of action? Among all the **red flags** listed here, remember: *This is the most important one.* How well a team disagrees is a sign of a high-performing team. No disagreement is not a positive sign—it is a **red flag**.

Inexperienced Staff

Not hiring the right people is setting yourself up for failure because inexperienced or incompetent staff *do not challenge their bosses.* As good people leave and inexperienced staff must be promoted, it is important to set up mechanisms such as training or mentoring programs to limit the consequences of their inexperience and ensure that they obtain the required skills quickly. Or, they must be closely managed by a hands-on manager/supervisor until their skills are up to par. This dynamic can certainly create a misstep for you and one that the rest of the organization, elected officials, and community won't forgive. This has increasingly become a **red flag** and a problem at all levels of the public sector, as recruitment and retention woes are worse than ever.

Unconsciously Competent

The last **red flag** is when you find yourself on autopilot in your position. This is different from incompetency. The authors who have studied this stage are conveying that this is when you are unconsciously competent and are no longer paying attention like you were when you started in the position. My concern is that this stage could lead to complacency for a public sector top-level leader. The authors of this concept, Curtiss and Warren,[13] describe the typical stages or learning chain as follows:

Four Stages of Adult Learning

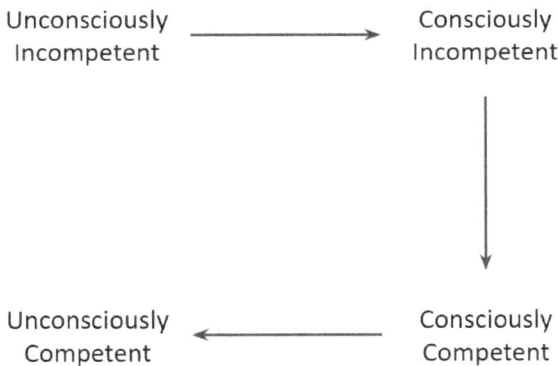

Unconsciously Incompetent	→	Consciously Incompetent
Unconsciously Competent	←	Consciously Competent

This diagram was created by Dick Bowers, a frequent guest presenter in leadership academies on subjects such as "Developing High Performing Teams". He used the work of Curtiss and Warren and their four stages of learning model to make the point that a top-level public sector leader cannot afford to be "Unconsciously Competent."

When leaders first step into a position, they are usually "unconsciously incompetent," which means that they pay attention to everything and realize that they don't know what they don't know. Then, they become "consciously incompetent," which means they begin to know what they don't know, so they work hard to become "consciously competent." This is the sweet spot. If they move to "unconsciously competent," they are on automatic pilot, like when driving the last two miles home from work on a path you know so well that you're barely aware that you are driving. The authors define this stage as the point where leaders have practiced their skills so much that they become intuitive or second nature. An intuitive skill is good, but engaging in autopilot in a high-level public sector leadership position is antithetical to the professional responsibilities of the role, given the constantly shifting daily variables. I would argue that leaders should always be thinking about "how the dominos will fall," like the top-level public leader, Mr. Astute Engineer, previously mentioned. So, unconscious competency means that a leader is not learning anymore; they are not noticing when the dynamics have changed, and they will likely miss the **red flags.**

Summary Remarks

Noticing the **red flags** is extraordinarily difficult because they are subtle and look a lot like things are going just fine until they aren't. How does a leader know that they aren't learning anymore when it could look a lot like unconscious competence? How does one notice that staff are not speaking up at the staff meetings, are withholding information you need to hear, or that they have given up trying to influence you because you don't listen carefully? To you, it may look like everyone is busy and just wants the staff meeting to end. How do you see ahead and realize that things are going to change in the structural arrangements in a way you cannot influence, that what is rewarding and challenging now will become intractable and even nasty? How do you recognize that the ratio of effort, anxiety, and stress is not worth it – that, as one top-level leader described, "…the deeply layered sense of accomplishment of the impact of the work is gone"?[14] If you have serious blind spots, how do you see a **red flag**? You might consider posting in your personal workspace the **red flags** outlined so that you periodically, take a close look and are forced to honestly assess your environment.

I am struck by the devious nature of rationalizations in discussing these **red flags** with others. A top-level leader will raise a **red flag** with me and say, "What do you think? Is this happening?" and then they spend their time trying to talk me out of what I think because the action it would take is not pleasing to them. This just happened a few months ago, and the top-level leader involved waited too long. Instead of being in front of the issue, she was reactive to it. She ignored her strong, undeniable sense that the vibes had gone bad between her and an elected official; too many battles later, she did not act to get out of the situation. The situation acted upon her instead. **Red flags** can slowly or quickly stop being **red flags** and lead to missteps, misjudgments, or scandals.

Endnotes

[1] Over the years, I have had numerous meetings, lunches, coffees, and debrief conversations about red flags and antidotes with top-level public sector leaders I have coached, so I could guide them on strategies. For the purposes of this book, I also interviewed a number of retired top-level public sector leaders to gather their thoughts on how and why their careers ended well.

[2] For a fuller description of this dynamic, see Collins (2009), pp. 36–42.

[3] Citation source confidential.

[4] Collins (2009), p. 45.

[5] Citation source confidential.

[6] Description of a DROP program taken from the website of the San Diego Retired Employees Association, City of San Diego (www.sdcers.org):

> "If you are eligible for a service retirement, but not quite ready to leave the workforce, DROP might be for you. DROP is a voluntary program that allows you to continue working for your plan sponsor for up to five years while simultaneously earning a monthly pension benefit. As long as you are still working for your plan sponsor, your monthly pension benefit will accumulate in a separate DROP account and earn interest. Once you actually retire and exit DROP, the money that has accrued in your DROP account will be paid to you, including interest, on top of your monthly pension benefit."

[7] Citation source confidential.

[8] Citation source confidential.

[9] Citation source confidential.

[10] Citation source confidential.

[11] Citation source confidential.

[12] This was an often-told scenario by Dick Bowers, former city manager of Scottsdale. Dick Bowers was a frequent guest speaker on "Building High-Performing Teams" during public sector leadership academies I facilitated between 1986 and 2017. He

recently passed away and will be terribly missed by the example he provided as a person of integrity. The stories he told were full of lessons for academy participants.

[13] In their book *The Dynamics of Life Skills Coaching* (1973), Curtis and Warren identify four stages of competence. Dick Bowers, (see above note) argued, as do I, that the fourth stage of competence in their model – "unconsciously competent" – can lead to complacency and missteps in the public sector.

[14] Citation source confidential.

Chapter Six

Antidotes and Mitigative Actions

There are numerous anticipatory actions and structures that a top-level public sector leader can put in place to protect, alert, or otherwise buffer them from making damaging mistakes that impact their careers, reputations, and/or legacies. Specifically, these antidotes might be able to prevent, relieve, counteract, or even cancel out the effects of a particularly bad situation. The focus of the antidotes listed in the following section is on counteracting, not curing, because there is no guarantee of a cure in a public sector environment. Specifically, the most important antidote is the artful act of anticipating, being aware of how one is perceived by others, minimizing the blind spots previously outlined, and being cognizant of the current context and structural arrangements, as well as the mindsets, beliefs, and skills one carries into a leadership position. When I asked Mr. Astute Engineer how he had successfully stayed out of trouble in the public arena, he said, "I never operated on the presumption I was right."[1]

Some of these antidotes directly respond to the red flags outlined in Chapter Five. Some suggestions can be implemented once a problem has already arisen and a graceful exit is required. Others are proposed as a way to ensure, from the start, a successful, challenging, and smooth career—one with complexity that requires all the skills in a leader's arsenal but also one without scandal or damage to an organization, a career, or a reputation.

The antidotes suggested were formulated following years of consulting with leaders and acquiring experience and knowledge from the rough and tumble of organizational life, observing what works and what does not work when taking mitigating actions, and establishing a well-honed theory and action. This particular chapter also weaves in data from interviews with those whose careers ended successfully, where they left at a high point, as hard as that is to do, or moved on to another organization when things looked troubling where they were. Their particular advice is noted and highlighted. These antidotes are presented in no particular order of priority.

Create Mechanisms to Signal to Yourself that It's Time to Leave

Develop professional benchmarks you want to reach, a set of accomplishments and/or goals, or put in place personal guideposts to direct your career and create a sense of when enough is enough. Mr. Wise and Noble Leader said this about his timing: "It was highly important to me to leave on top...I accomplished everything I wanted to accomplish. It was time, and I have never once regretted it. I knew it was right."[2] While he was heavily lobbied to stay, he stuck with his decision largely due to his analysis and clarity of what he had already accomplished, what he saw ahead that concerned him, and his values about how he wanted to close the loop on his public sector career.

Another successful retired top-level public sector leader respected for his expertise spent several decades in various positions navigating the water business, which is fraught with infighting between agencies and board members who sometimes stay so long that they die in their seats. When I debriefed him about his retirement decision, he said that he had a list of what he wanted to accomplish when he accepted the top-level position. Reflecting on the list, he realized he had done it all. He had created a solid executive team that had not existed previously, he had set up the next generation of leaders, he had made changes to the retirement system that would benefit employees, he had stabilized the budget for years to come, and he had focused on long-term maintenance needs.

His reason for focusing on this list was that he was experiencing a lot of resistance and critique from a new board member. This leader realized that this situation was not going to change because there was a collection of citizens who followed and supported this new board member, and active blogging was going on between them. A new day had come to his agency. He knew his role was going to change. The focus of attention was going to shift from producing positive outcomes within this high-performing agency to attacks on the agency's executive leadership and him specifically. He knew that this kind of dynamic creates tension regarding vision, direction, and management decisions, which erodes the effectiveness of the organization. This was not a fate he wanted, and it was predictable. So, he retired with a fabulous legacy, a happy and joyful celebration, and the satisfaction of a career well-spent.[3]

These goals were meaningful to this leader but there can be other guideposts to pay attention to. It is helpful for leaders to reflect periodically on their attitudes and frames of mind about the positions they hold. I urge you to take the time to stand back and look at yourself from outside yourself. If in your early or mid-career, do you have the desire to work in an environment that is more difficult and complex, or smaller or bigger? Are you feeling like things are getting too complex, and a mistake is inevitable because you are finding it increasingly difficult to manage all the variables? Are there upcoming changes in the city council, board, or the platform the elected official ran on to get elected that cause you concern? Are you finding that the elected officials or the leaders above you are starting to blame you or lose confidence in you as a result of citizen complaints and dissatisfaction? One top-level public leader, Ms. Go-To, Get-It-Done Leader, told me during an interview about her career that she began to seriously feel the absence of her mentor, her previous boss, who always had her back. Her "get-it-done" approach had typically had the support from above and she was usually able to win over the elected officials as well because she and her boss were a united front. Since her boss/mentor's departure, she was observing the cool reception she was getting from the new leader who took his place and thought it might be time to leave. Her influence and risk-taking had always gone better when she had that solid support above her, and she suspected this would change for the worse in this new environment, and she would be left holding the bag anytime something went south with the community or between departments and agencies. She was a star, but the signs were that her star shined too bright next to the new leader above her.[4] There are many leaders who have "protectors" who go to bat for them, who "save their bacon" in a tough situation. They may not have been a mentor to the top-level public sector leader, but they are champions in the business community, union leadership, well-known community leaders or elected officials. If they have been a backer of yours, and they have moved on and are no longer in your world, your environment has changed for you in ways that Ms. Go-to, Get-it-Done described for herself.

There is a tendency in the public sector to think leaving means something is wrong, or someone is in trouble. However, leaving may, in fact, be what is best not only for the leader making the decision to leave but also for the organization, given the changing environment and what it would take to stay in it – to stay in it with influence. That is why this is a mitigative action.

A top-level public sector leader, Ms. Savvy Leader, said that her internal compass or her time-to-leave mechanism was essentially her morality. She had a good sense of right and wrong. Attributing this to her upbringing and early religious learnings, she immediately knew when something she was being asked to do or was being asked to be a part of was not for the public good and crossed a line. While she worked, sometimes successfully and sometimes not, to get others to see the problem with their approach or request, she felt her guidepost was that she was "never afraid to be fired or to quit" for refusing to carry out what she was being asked to do. Consequently, her mitigative action was to move to different city organizations every few years. Her moral compass never hurt her ability to be hired elsewhere because she was competent, thorough, and a true leader. Her intentions were clear, and she felt that leaving was a "good thing" and not a bad thing.[5] Going out at the top of your game is the best possible scenario, and if moving to another position for a variety of reasons or deciding to retire if at or near the end of your career achieves this end, then seriously consider this. Building in time to reflect and take stock is an important structure and action leaders can put in place.

Ms. Savvy Leader, who felt leaving was a good thing, provided one further insight. She stated that she was willing to be fired because she knew it would likely be over an ethical issue. Thus, she felt that violations of her bottom line were always the result of an ethical issue. This comfort with the idea of being fired is rare among public sector leaders and is typically voiced only by those who are close to retirement and have the confidence they could influence those above them because "they know I could quit at any time." Quitting or resigning on the basis of an ethical dilemma, however, is significantly less impactful to an organization than a leader getting fired. I always think the impact on the organization needs to be factored in. However, being comfortable with getting fired is an important antidote for one to consider and requires the unique clarity to know your bottom line. This concept was reinforced by Mr. Wise and Noble Leader, who said, "You can't fear for your job...you need to understand this from the get-go.... I told my board, I am not afraid to lose my job."[6] This leader felt that the statement made a tangible impression on his board about his character. While debriefing with a retired top-level public sector leader about what influenced his thinking regarding when and how to step out of the top city manager role, he reminded me that he had been a mentee of Mr. Wise and Noble Leader and was heavily influenced by his counsel many years prior, when he was advised, "there is no job worth your reputation."

It is important to note that the advice given in this chapter, and throughout the book, about getting in front of missteps and knowing how to manage them does not take into account the economic hardships involved. Not everyone can afford to move to another jurisdiction for a new position or to retire. Social class, personal economic circumstances, and the double-bind of work/family inevitably influence the decisions we make at certain times in our careers and lives.

Build Your "Bank Account"

Any top-level public sector leader should have an exquisite understanding of the notion of giving more than you take and building your "bank account" with others by coming through for them and knowing that obligations and debts matter. Therefore, when leaders make a mistake or need to make a request, they have a bank account or currency to draw from. This is critically important for successfully surviving a misstep or making a substantial request. A bank account gives leaders degrees of freedom to take risks and/or protects them during a mistake, but only if they, in turn, do this for others and have done so over time. This is an iterative process, and leaders must never stop working at or take it for granted.

If you are a high-maintenance leader—that is, you require a lot of social interaction to assure yourself that you are doing a good job—you can quickly use up your bank account, so you better have a big one. If you have too many burned bridges, your bank account is probably overdrawn. This is something that you work hard to build, and though no one ever talks about it, you can use it up with a serious mistake or a highly public misstep. Then, you need to build it back up if you are going to expect to maintain your influence at the highest levels. No one will ever tell you they are keeping score, but they absolutely are. The scorecard can last for years. They may not cash it in, or you may not cash it in very often, but it is understood that it exists at the highest levels. It is expected that you will absolutely understand this. Always give more than you take. When you need help or a favor, if you have built up enough of a bank account and have come through enough for other people, you can make the ask with the expectation that you will need to come through for others to build it up again. Withdrawing from your bank account is an antidote—a mitigative action you can take to protect yourself in most cases, depending on the context, type of misstep, and/or scandal.

This was brought home to me during an interview with a retired small city top-level leader, Ms. Solid-Track-Record, who always had administrative functions reporting to her, like human resources, finance, risk management, and purchasing. She had established, over many, many years, in some difficult city organizations, a solid track record of coming through. Her role, and how she did her role, had put her in the position to have accumulated many "I owe you one" or "you saved me on this one" IOU's. Numerous times, she and her staff had saved the day with last-minute creative solutions, research, or burning the midnight oil reports. This gave her degrees of freedom to counter and push back on a request from above or a policy decision about to be made that she felt crossed the ethical line for her or was not wise for the organization. This is how she maintained her moral compass in many complex and highly political situations. She used her bank account. She retired without scandal or incident.[7]

Think Several Steps Ahead

It is important to stress the importance of being farsighted and seeing what is coming from all directions. More than one top-level leader who exited successfully said to me, "I saw ahead and realized it wasn't going to be fun anymore." While these leaders threw out the word "fun", they each meant something far deeper and meaningful than "fun". They saw the political winds, the new players, the change in structural arrangements, and they saw the battles ahead. On top of being farsighted, leaders need to have a peripheral vision where they can anticipate what isn't necessarily ahead in a logical way but what might come from side skirmishes or detours that are likely to impact their environments.

Thus, leaders must step outside themselves and their self-interests and look honestly and clearly down the road about what is likely coming from the larger context—nationally or internationally—that they can't even see yet. I recommend doing this when you least feel like it. Anticipating what might happen is also how you can take steps toward improvement while ensuring that something bad doesn't happen. For example, one top-level public sector leader knew he was going to be second-guessed by the chief of staff coming in with a new mayoral administration. He knew the reputation of the incoming chief of staff and had faced an earlier exchange that felt like a directive versus a suggestion, so he moved on to another position before he was asked to do something he was not willing, ethically, to do. He took a mitigative action to avoid a potential line in the sand or a public standoff.[8]

At numerous points from 2004 to 2006, I witnessed dozens of top-level public sector leaders resign from their positions and seek out comparable positions throughout their region and in other regions. The city government they had worked for had transitioned from a city council/manager form of government to a strong mayor form of government. They anticipated that this charter change, voted on by citizens, might compromise their roles in ways they could not abide. Top-level leaders in other jurisdictions throughout the country regularly discuss with their colleagues at annual conferences the impact of a change in tone, values, and norms once newly elected officials come on their city councils, boards of supervisors, water boards, and the like. These ripple effects from elections, citizen initiatives, and state or federally imposed mandates are an opportunity for top-level leaders to look ahead and reflect on what the impact might be. Only then can they decide whether they want to get ahead of this or wait to see what happens and be prepared to respond in ways that protect one's job satisfaction, reputation, and career.

Create a Devil's Advocate Role

Any high-performing team simply must discuss the undiscussable. This might be one of the most important antidotes. As mentioned previously, too often in my research, I found teams in which no one had the courage or relationship to tell the leader the truth. Top-level public leaders *must have a right-hand person who tells them the truth*. This can be a staff member at any level. However, I urge you to select someone who will let you know you are walking off a cliff or, when you seem to have lost your way, someone who knows you well enough to let you know you are no longer acting on your "true north," and someone who will tell you that you're embroiled in a misstep *when you're in it*, not after the fact. It does you no good to have your right-hand person say in the aftermath of a scandal, "I knew this was going to get you in trouble." It is simply not possible to say that you have a true team around you when not one of them would be willing to call you out if need be. If they try and you ignore them, that's one thing, but if they don't try, this is truly problematic. You must build this high-performing team with members who have the skills and courage to tell the truth, who have your back, and vice versa. It might even behoove you to build a team smarter than you. I recommend rewarding and structuring your team as early as possible. To do this, practice debate with no retaliation, practice advocacy for other points of view, and practice good inquiry before you need it. Once a serious misstep pops up, things get fuzzy, and often, normal communication shuts down. Then, it becomes too late to try to create a team.

Develop the skills of good advocacy and good inquiry within the team, too.[9] Good advocacy includes team members saying what they think and their rationale for their thinking. Then, they ask you what you think of what they said. Good inquiry requires asking more questions to improve understanding than making statements. Both are required for a high-performing team. Leaders must exemplify this themselves and be role models for what they expect of others.

Furthermore, learn about your team's EQ. Greaves and Watkins (2021) applied their previous work on one's personal EQ to create high-performing teams with good EQ. For example, you can use your personal EQ to learn how your team members react to emotions that surface in team meetings and how this gets in the way, specifically, of speaking the truth to the leader. This is a critical insight that can help your team speak up.[10]

Clarify for your team that you see a difference between naysayers and thoughtful leaders. Naysayers can't be satisfied. Thoughtful leaders are people who disagree and can be persuaded, or they can persuade you. Do not label those who disagree with you as naysayers. This could cause you to replicate the O-ring dynamic that occurred during the decision-making before the Challenger flight. The engineer who voiced concerns was labeled a naysayer, but he was actually a team player and a thoughtful leader. Consequently, his advice not to launch at temperatures too low as the O-rings would not hold was not taken. The dialogue that led to the decision has been reenacted and shows the centrality of credible advocacy, the danger of labeling, and the team's reaction to the emotion in the room.[11] It is the fault of both the engineer for not having been an effective advocate (he was seen as a "crying wolf" too often) and the leader of that team for labeling a knowledgeable engineer serving a valuable role of being a critic or challenger, as a naysayer. The leaders missed the warning signs by not listening closely. To ensure that a critique and a serious warning are discernible, a leader must listen, and the team must make their points well. Given that the topic here is missteps and scandals, top-level public sector leaders should err on the side of caution and listen closely, even when subordinates are not speaking up effectively. The cost of not doing so is a misstep or a critical mistake from which one may not recover.

Ms. Solid-Track- Record had an insightful take on why this devil's advocate dynamic was indispensable to her effectiveness: "As we move up, we move further from the thing we were trained to do like being an engineer or a budget analyst...eventually you oversee areas you never worked in. You have to learn to trust your experts and not feel like you have to know it all...you eventually lose the technical chops. The field keeps evolving. I always told my teams that I relied on them to be the technical experts and actively encouraged them to challenge me. I would say, I don't need you guys to tell me I'm brilliant. I need you to tell me where I'm wrong. I am not trying to be the smartest person in the room."[12]

There is always the possibility of team members who do speak up and speak up loudly, and the leader ignores their advice. It is hard to imagine that there were no staff who challenged the pension obligation strategy at one of the big city public organizations I referenced (in Chapter One) or who questioned the big city Real Estate Deal's lease-to-own decision or the decision to move staff into the building too early. Furthermore, competent staff must have provided well-stated arguments at the big city RTA about the questionable future cost projections of the transportation initiative. And someone must have dissented against a big city school board chair who violated her role by stepping into the administrative side of the house to direct counselors and teachers by passing the superintendent (see Appendix B, Mario Koran 2016 article on big city school board). And surely, HR staff must have questioned the directive to move women staff out of a high-profile state governor's office suite to protect them from potential advances rather than deal with the governor's behavior directly. A devil's advocate may have been present in all situations, and the issue might have been that the leadership repeatedly did not listen.

Slow Down: Rely on System 2 Decision-Making

Within the field of systems thinking and its overlap with ethics research on cognitive limitations is the notion that System 1 decision-making is rushed and based on intuitive thinking. It is fast, emotional, quick, and effortless. System 2 decision-making is slower, conscious, explicit, logical, and requires effort. If done right, System 2 thinking involves making comparisons when evaluating actions and looking at multiple options. The deliberative approach of System 2 thinking leads to more ethical behaviors and better decisions.[13] This is a mitigative action that a savvy top-level public sector leader should practice when contemplating the next steps when facing a misstep or scandal.

Manage Your Reaction to Ambiguity

Some of us can sit with ambiguity or gray areas, and some of us cannot. Urged by anxiety or worry, we must act, as any action is perceived as better than none. Knowing what triggers you and having this self-awareness is important insight so that you can self-manage your behavior and act in a thoughtful and conscious manner. This is related to the concept of EQ frequently referenced in this book[14] and is worth reading to increase your skills in the area. Self-awareness is important here, but it is the self-management piece of this advice that will keep you from making a misstep.

Be on the "Praiseworthy" Side of the "Blame Continuum"

When a mistake or scandal happens, causing embarrassment for the top-level public sector leader's organization, it is important to understand what happened and tell the truth about it; was it a mistake that deserves blame, or was it a praiseworthy mistake? In the public sector, we have a tendency to treat all mistakes the same because they are picked up by the media. Note in the continuum below that not all mistakes are equal.[15]

"Blame/Praise" Continuum
A Spectrum of Reasons for Mistakes
(not all mistakes are equal):

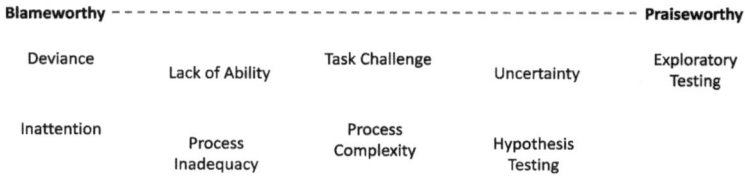

Blameworthy - Praiseworthy

| Deviance | | Task Challenge | | Exploratory Testing |
| Lack of Ability | | Uncertainty |

| Inattention | | Process Complexity | | |
| Process Inadequacy | | Hypothesis Testing |

Continuum developed by Sopp, T., 2014; concepts taken from a Harvard Business Review article by Amy C. Edmond, "Strategies for Learning From Failure," *Harvard Business Review*, *89*(4), 2011, and formatted here as a continuum.

A **deviance mistake** (i.e., it was calculated, intended to do harm, outside the norms, or illegal) is one deserving of blame. Consider, for example, the big city school board chair who pressured the superintendent of the school system to approve a financial settlement involving a lawsuit the chair's son brought over the content of his college letters of recommendation. Another example is the big city mayor, who used his position of power to intimidate women in the office with his sexual overtures. Both scenarios constitute deviance mistakes.

Mistakes such as inattention to detail, miscalculation of numbers, or failure to proofread a contract are **blameworthy mistakes**. However, mistakes made because a process improvement did not work or was not on the mark or because a new fuel plan for trucks did not yield the desired results are **less blameworthy.**

The mayor of a small city who apologized to his constituents about a water "shut off" problem and handed out bottled water in contrition did not fire any staff but made getting bottled water to residents a priority. As such, this was not as blameworthy. However, further investigation revealed this to be a water system set-up and maintenance problem (i.e., good water and bad water pipes co-mingled in a problematic way due to a rope that had fallen into the system) that had a long history and should never have happened. Thus, this constitutes a **process inadequacy.** The mayor was further able to get through this scandal by not throwing others under the bus. If he had knowingly voted against the staff's recommended process improvements to improve the water flow system, this would have been **blameworthy.**

Blame in the public arena is nearly always about who did it or who is at fault. However, a mistake made in an attempt to improve a process or structure where testing and experimentation are being done without incurring too much of a cost is a **praiseworthy mistake**.

A city council's or board of supervisors' role in how blame is assigned at city hall or, a county government, or any board of a public agency is significant. This assignment of blame is a particularly devastating behavior that impacts an entire public organization, no matter how big or small. Just the notion that any mistake will be met with the question, "Who did it?" is anxiety-inducing and can damage morale.

Think for a moment how connected the behavior of, for example, the city council, board of supervisors, or water board is to the work environments of top-level public sector leaders and their entire workforce. The behavior of elected officials who sit at the top of public sector organizations is more central to their top-level public sector leader's productivity than it is to the community and community groups, which do not notice every nuance, slight, and signal made from the dais.

Staff spend an enormous amount of time interpreting an interruption, a sarcastic joke, a side conversation, or a raised eyebrow made by an elected official. Elected officials need to understand this thoroughly and completely and self-manage their behaviors, or if the actions are intentional, explain them. Furthermore, it is also incumbent on the staff to figure them out.

However, when it comes to placing blame about a mistake that hit the front page of the paper or was trending on social media, public sector elected officials have a particular responsibility for how they react. Typically, the focus is on the mistake and finding someone to blame for it rather than on the problem that needs to be solved. In other words, "How do we make sure this doesn't happen again?" is a problem-oriented focus. Ms. Solid Track Record knew this well and had the bank account to change the question. When the focus is on who is to blame, a reinforcing loop occurs. Blame can lead staff to look around at each other and quietly make accusations while being fearful of losing their jobs. When public sector staff are not talking to each other to solve problems, this leads to more mistakes, divisiveness, a lack of confidence, an unwillingness to share information about the mistake and the issues involved, and a shutdown of risk-taking because staff members are fearful, which leads to more mistakes and ultimately more blame.

Mental Models and Mind Sets: Reinforcing Cycle of Blame

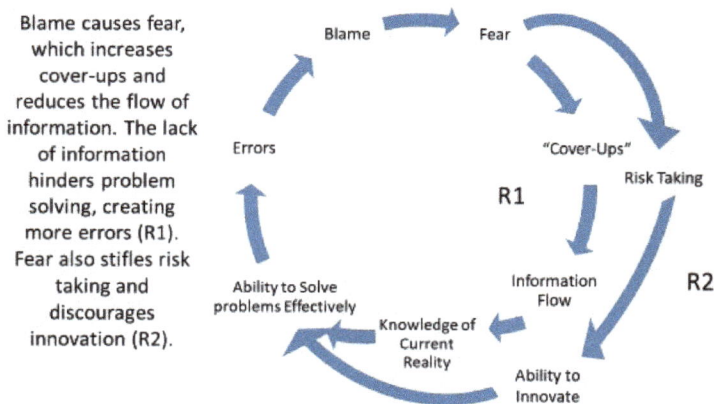

Blame causes fear, which increases cover-ups and reduces the flow of information. The lack of information hinders problem solving, creating more errors (R1). Fear also stifles risk taking and discourages innovation (R2).

Blame · Fear · "Cover-Ups" · Risk Taking · R1 · R2 · Errors · Information Flow · Ability to Solve problems Effectively · Knowledge of Current Reality · Ability to Innovate

Taken from Marilyn Paul, Systems Thinker, Vol. 8, No. 1.

Taken from Marilyn Paul, **Systems Thinker,**
Volume 8, No.1.

The classic mental model and mindset for reinforcing the cycle of blame developed by Marilyn Paul for the *Systems Thinker* newsletter describes what happens during the blame-placing cycle.[16] Public sector staff know that their morale is not the number one concern of the elected official body. Staff job satisfaction should be the focus of their direct supervisor or manager. Typically, elected officials are most concerned with what their constituents think and what the interest groups who got them elected want. Those constituents and individual interest groups elected these officials to create policy, and that's the job of elected officials.

There is a clear connection between servicing constituents well and the organization's psyche. My message to elected officials is that there's a better solution than blame. Problem-solving rather than blame-placing will bring you better results.

Regarding the public sector leader who knows very well that blame is a frequent reaction by elected officials and citizens in a political environment, akin to a fishbowl, many a top-level public sector leader is trying to survive the ambiguity of where the mistake falls along the blameworthy and praiseworthy continuum: if you feel you have gotten labeled as a "poor decision-maker" since the incident occurred or there is now a question mark about your judgment that is verbalized or inferred by others, this can be turned around if you want to stay and do the work to turn it around. This requires an immediate, 180-degree change in whatever behavior led to the misstep.

Perhaps you did not do a thorough review when the work was forwarded to you. Or you did not ask the important questions. Or you depended on others when the stakes were high and did not provide clear direction in your absence. Or you took a shortcut in your oversight, as this was a mistake you would have found if you had paid closer attention. Or you simply missed the politics completely. If you immediately, and without rationalizations, act differently because you understand what you missed the first time out, and you, for example, consistently adopt this new behavior of closer oversight or clearer and more timely communication with the staff about context or the stakes, or you better grasp the political environment, and these insights and behaviors are obvious to others, you can often reverse the label with time. It is very hard once labeled to change a label, yet *it can be done* but only with sincere and consistent behavioral change that is noticeable, not subtle, and your ownership of this new behavior is clear to yourself and your bosses, colleagues, and team. Any perceived rationalizations will doom you with the elected officials, community, and your staff.

Reframe the Issue…as Larger

It is important for leaders to determine how to incorporate all interests and situate a controversial issue within a *larger context from a different perspective*. To do this, they must make the umbrella for the issue *larger*. This requires listening well and seriously thinking about the solution, action, or way of thinking that sees the problem as a challenge to solve so that the solution can incorporate more interests than your own (e.g., your department's needs, the city council's or board's interests, community interests, and/or even regional and statewide interests).[17]

There was a particular big city agency top-level public sector leader, Ms. Big Picture Thinker, who did this brilliantly. She was a harsh leader at times, but when it came to her board, she could really see the biggest picture possible.[18] She knew how the discussion should be structured to get at a solution that incorporated as many of their constituents' interests as possible and turned the problem from a burden into a challenge to solve it in the most inclusive way possible or with the most wins possible. This is a highly important skill—a practiced way of thinking that requires getting outside of the situation. It is impressive to see this skill in action, and self-discipline is required to ensure that it is consistently applied in all situations. Evidence of how hard this is includes the crucial times when she did not employ this skill when she was blinded by her stake in the ground, or when she was swayed by the potential for a win or just personally too invested, and this very skill set was nowhere to be found. I urge you to pay attention; know who or what is aiming to get its hooks in you, know your personal vulnerabilities and in what situations they are likely to cause you to behave inappropriately.

When is the Right thing the Wrong thing?

Words and beliefs like "right," "wrong," "duty," "true north," or "never give up" are powerful messages that can clarify things and tip the dynamic, providing the direction that employees want. Identifying the right direction is especially important in complex situations.

It is honorable to lead a team, even during a lost-cause project, and take responsibility for the fall. However, at what point does the "never give up" value flip? That is, at what point does "never give up" change to "we have to give up now before we lose more or cost the organization more resources?"

Part of being great is knowing when to step back and admit that a project is not going to work—to say, "We need to end it now" and admit the mistake. This blind spot may be caused by the desire to win, score one for your efforts, or best someone else, which is exactly the wrong thing to do with the community or with the elected body. Letting go of the value proposition "to win at any cost" takes insight and more discipline and commitment than staying the course right off the cliff.

Another source of self-discipline is to be willing to walk away from the power inherent in a position. In an interview with a top-level public sector leader, he expressed that he was perplexed about one particular colleague who was clearly in danger of exiting on a sour note, but this colleague could not see this. His conclusion was that his colleague "just could not give up the power of the position," that the ability to "snap your fingers" and make something happen is addicting, and that "it takes a lot to walk away from it."[19] My question to the reader is: What does "it takes a lot to walk away from it" mean? What does power, winning, and never giving up mean when juxtaposed with character, vision of the future, self-discipline, confidence, and the valuing of one's reputation? Conflicting values are at the heart of most ethical dilemmas. Thus, it is worth reflecting on what one's values are at critical points in one's career. I watched Ms. Go-To, Get-It-Done Leader, a talented and beloved top-level public sector leader, retire younger than most and confidently walk out the door to an adoring crowd of admirers for exactly this reason. Her self-respect and good reputation intact.

Finally, it is clear that recent national social issues have influenced the type of leadership style and values required to be successful in the public, private, and non-profit sectors alike. What must be part of your focus as a leader and should be forefront in your mind are equity and equality issues raised by the social justice movement; equity and social value issues raised during the COVID-19 pandemic and the communities impacted most by it; the #MeToo movement highlighting demeaning, illegal, and offensive behaviors previously considered a norm; LGBTQ+ issues surrounding inclusion and acceptance; generational differences in workplace leadership and values; the rights and concerns of the differently abled; designing workplaces that respect remote or hybrid work. These are just a few of the diversity, equity, and inclusion topics and workforce concerns swirling in organizations and larger society. Being sensitive, aware, adaptable, forward-thinking, caring and sympathetic to these social and workplace issues is a prerequisite for a competent and effective leader in these times. If this is not you, if you are impatient with these demands and beliefs, and if you do not have the interest or passion to be responsive to these issues, then it is time to step out of the top-level public sector leadership role.

Know How to Exit Gracefully

If exiting is the right direction or the mitigative action that needs to take place, then make your exit smooth. Make it a project. Think about the steps with some detachment. Here are some questions to ask yourself and issues to consider about timing and the course of action to take:

- Assess your situation: What is coming up? What could blow up? What has happened to your colleagues in other jurisdictions as they have tried to depart? What don't you see that others see?

- Put down a date and toss it around in your head as you consider the answers to the questions.

- Determine the strengths and skills of your team and capitalize on them as they handle your departure.

- Assess your board or council dynamics; imagine who might insist you stay and your response to this. What might the media do, and who will handle and respond to what they say and write?

- Think through the internal/external successor issue and your recommendations.

- Lay out the pros and cons of the timing of your announcement. Anticipate you might be asked to stay on as a special advisor or subcontractor. Be prepared to respond to this request so that you are not caught agreeing to something. In the absence of a graceful out, you might be stuck doing something you don't want to do.

- Map the potential political dynamics as a result of your announcement. Ask yourself who will do what, when, and what do I need to get in front of? What should I say, and in what order?

- Think through what you would need to put in place to remain the top-level public sector leader until you depart. What is your role in the transition? How big of an influence do you want to have in what happens next? Do you want a role in the selection process? Whether it is advisable to stay out of it completely depends on the context, but most top-level leaders who get involved in some way regret it, as the responsibility shifts to them, and it is hard to extricate themselves out of the transition even once the selection is made.

- Ceremonies are good; they provide closure and normalize the process of departing. Think about what you want to do to host a goodbye gathering for your colleagues and staff. Be generous, and remember, you have much to thank them for, and they will want to thank you.

When it comes to their own departure, many successful top-level public sector leaders get muddy in their thinking, sentimental in their feelings, and self-deceptive in their thoughts. Analytical skills go out the door. Sometimes, passive-aggressive behaviors take place based on past resentments. At this junction, it is important to get a personal grip on this issue and take control. It is your final duty as a leader. You must leave the organization clear, not confused, hopeful, not sad, and ready, not anxious.

Summary Remarks

There is an undeniable maturity required to implement the antidotes and mitigative actions outlined in this chapter. One cannot be trying to settle a score or one- up someone else or leave in order to embarrass one's boss. The suggestions offered require the truest of intentions to work. Whether it is to stay and build one's bank account, reframe an issue for even greater insight, step back, take the hit, and reassess what you are really trying to do after all, or exit when the time is right for you. These are all good and noble actions in the best interests of the public sector. Become familiar with them so you know there are definitive ways to bounce back from a misstep, misjudgment, or even a scandal. Become familiar with them so you can tweak them to your liking. Timing matters. They can time out and then are no longer effective. If you try to build your bank account, when you have dipped into it so often, with the same sorts of mistakes, you have timed out. If you finally see the light that your "we're in it until the end" mindset is a mistake, well after too much damage has been done, you have timed out. Become familiar with how to bounce back from a misstep hardship before you need it, and know that when to hold'em and when to fold'em is an option for you, too. The options in this chapter should become familiar ground to you.

Endnotes

[1] Citation source confidential.

[2] Citation source confidential.

[3] Citation source confidential.

[4] Citation source confidential.

[5] Citation source confidential.

[6] Citation source confidential.

[7] Citation source confidential.

[8] Citation source confidential.

[9] For helpful resources to create an environment where staff speak up, see "Team Learning" in Senge (1994), Patterson et al. (2002), and Lencioni (2002).

[10] See *Team Emotional Intelligence 2.0,* by Greaves & Watkins (2021). Specifically, see Chapters Five ("Emotional Awareness Strategies") and Six ("Emotional Management Strategies").

[11] Watch the reenactment of the entire dialogue between management and engineers in the NASA launch decision in *Groupthink, Revised Edition* by CRM Films (1998).

[12] Citation source confidential.

[13] Kahneman (2011).

[14] See all emotional intelligence books by Dr. Jean Greaves listed in the Bibliography.

[15] See Edmond (2011), "Strategies for Learning From Failure." Also, for a discussion about failure, see Birkinshow & Haas (2016), "Increase Your Return on Failure."

[16] See any article in the *Systems Thinker* newsletters but in particular the seminal article by Marilyn Paul (1997), "Moving from Blame to Accountability." Every elected official should read this article.

[17] For more on reframing, read "Using Framing to Face a Challenge" from the 2005 *Leader to Leader* newsletter.

[18] Citation source confidential.

[19] Citation source confidential.

Conclusion

As I bring this book to a close, I want to again express the deep respect I have for the public sector profession and its leaders. The degree of difficulty top-level leaders face as they make important and consequential decisions in the service of citizens and communities throughout this country can neither be overstated nor fully appreciated. This book and its candid, tough observations aim to support and further your work and mission.

While completing numerous final administrative book details, I paused to take one last snapshot of some of the publicly reported missteps, misjudgments, and scandals in the western region of the country during a five-month period in mid-2023. During this brief period, the following occurred:

- A college system chancellor was forced to resign because of mishandling investigations and ignoring complaints.

- The chair of a big county board of supervisors resigned his position due to an "improper" relationship that became contentious and public.

- The public sector leader of a big city port was put on administrative leave during an investigation that was never clarified, and soon after, a port board member was censured for misconduct.

- A top-level public sector leader in a medium-sized city resigned immediately after investigation results confirmed evidence of his sexual harassment of numerous staff.

- As calls for his resignation grew at each board meeting, Mr. Controversial Visionary offered his resignation while detailing accomplishments during his tenure and admitting his relationship with his board had been "strained."

- An ex-dean of a big city university pleaded guilty to bribing an elected official. The offender, in this case, is quoted as saying, "I think I would never imagine that in a career of 50 years, the culmination point would be a judgment of wrongdoing." The judge agreed, stating, "It is unfortunate that such an illustrious career comes to an end (in this way)."[1]

These too-frequent, sometimes tragic, incidences of career-shattering missteps, misjudgments, or scandals continue with long-term consequences that are harmful to the very citizens and communities that public sector leaders are dedicated to serving.

For those who feel the concepts, examples, and warning signs in this book are not applicable to them, I ask you to pause and consider, and then reconsider again, the nature of your circumstances, especially in high-profile projects with significant public consequences. You can learn the hard way or you can take seriously that as the complexity of your work continues to grow, the concepts presented in this book are more applicable than ever. As previously stated, even when some top-level public sector leaders are expertly and explicitly advised of relevant blind spots and likely potential missteps, these leaders insist that they are the exception and that this information is not applicable to them. By the time they realize they are not an exception, it is too late. The damage is done, a public sector career impacted, a legacy destroyed.

It takes uncommon self-discipline to do the sort of reflection and taking stock before acting that I am asking of you. To keep your eyes wide open and leave "nothing to chance" is a high bar. Yet I want and expect nothing less than this of public sector professionals and leaders. I want you to "…leave it all on the field" professionally and do so without suffering or subjecting others to the harmful consequences identified in these pages. I want you to realize the "true north" of your contributions as a public sector leader and to see it clearly, without any diminishing misstep. I want your careers to be, without qualification, worthy of celebration, where you enjoy the immense satisfaction that comes with a job well-done, a community well served, with few regrets.

The impact of missteps, misjudgments, and scandals chronicled in this book are presented with the goal that you, the top-level public sector leader, consciously manage your career in an intentional and optimally effective manner, especially when it is most difficult to do so whether you are at the beginning, middle, or end of your career. That you have a renewed appreciation for the serious, increasingly complex, and dynamic challenges that face public sector leaders and a frank assessment of what this requires and demands of you. The stakes in your work have always been high, and now they are even higher. It is never too late to be rigorous with yourself about the **red flags,** to take the **red flags** seriously, and to incorporate the suggested antidotes and mitigative actions where necessary.

As a citizen who enjoys the benefits of your public service each day, it has been a privilege to work with and support you in your efforts to better serve the public.

Endnotes

[1] Associated Press. (2023, July 25).

Bibliography

Ammerman, C., Groysberg, B., & Rometty, G. (2023). The new-collar workforce. *Harvard Business Review, 101*(2), 96.

Aratani, L. (2021, August 3). Andrew Cuomo Sexual Harassment: The Key Testimony from the Report. *The Guardian.*

Archie, A. (2022, September 14). Andrew Cuomo files a complaint against Letitia James for her sexual harassment report. *NPR.*

Argyris, C. (1990). *Overcoming Organizational Defenses.* London, UK: Pearson.

Associated Press. (2023, July 25). Ex-USC Dean Sentenced to Home Confinement. *Los Angeles Times.*

Badaracco, Jr., J. (1997). *Defining Moments: When Managers Must Choose between Right and Right.* Boston, MA: Harvard Business School Press.

Bazerman, M.H. (2022). *Complicit: How We Enable the Unethical and How to Stop.* Princeton, NJ: Princeton University Press.

Bazerman, M.H. & Tenbrunsel, A.E. (2013). *Blind Spots: Why We Fail to Do What's Right and What to Do About It.* Princeton, NJ: Princeton University Press.

Birkinshow, J. & Haas, M. (2016, May). Increase Your Return on Failure. *Harvard Business Review, 94,* 88-93.

Boardman, J.T. & Sauser, B. (2008). *Systems Thinking: Coping with 21st Century Problems.* Boca Raton, FL: CRC Press.

Bolino, M. & Phelps, C. (2023, January-February). Should Employees Be Allowed to Work Remotely Even If Others Can't? *Harvard Business Review, 101*(1), 144.

Bowen, A. (2017, August 8). SANDAG Executive Gary Gallegos to Retire Amid Scandal. *KPBS.*

Bowman, J. (2023, January 19). SANDAG's Divided Board Off to a Rocky Year After Small City Walkout. *Voice of San Diego.*

Bradberry, T. & Greaves, J. (2005). *The Emotional Intelligence Quick Book.* New York, NY: Simon and Schuster.

Bradberry, T. & Greaves, J. (2009). *Emotional Intelligence 2.0.* San Diego, CA: TalentSmart.

Bradberry, T. & Greaves, J. (2012). *Leadership 2.0.* San Diego, CA: TalentSmart.

Buckingham, M. (2022, May-June). Designing Work That People Love, *Harvard Business Review, 100(3),* 66-75.

Cavanaugh, M., Patiño, H., & Bracken, A. (2023, April 11*). Fletcher Controversy is One in a Long Line of Democrat Sex Scandals* [Audio podcast]. KPBS Midday Edition.

Charmaz, K. (2006). *Constructing Grounded Theory: A Practical Guide through Qualitative Analysis.* Thousand Oaks, CA: Sage Publications, Inc.

Collins J. (2009). *Why The Mighty Fall: And Why Some Companies Never Give In.* New York, NY: Harper Collins.

Cosgrove, J. (2019, March 17). Super bloom shutdown: Lake Elsinore shuts access after crowds descend on poppy fields. *Los Angeles Times.*

Creswell, J.W. & Poth, C.N. (2017). *Qualitative Inquiry and Research Design: Choosing Among Five Approaches* (4th Edition). Thousand Oaks, CA: Sage Publications, Inc.

Curtiss, P.R. & Warren, P. (1973). *The Dynamics of Life Skills Coaching.* Prince Albert, Sask., Canada: Training Research and Development Station, Department of Manpower and Immigration.

Derrington, M. L. (2019). *Qualitative Longitudinal Methods: Researching Implementation and Change.* Thousand Oaks, CA: Sage Publications, Inc.

Editorial Board. (2017, October 13). Revamped SANDAG Won't Rebuild Trust Quickly After Its Credibility Crumbled. *The San Diego Union-Tribune.*

Editorial Board. (2022, April 16). Blithe Spending of Public Funds Shows Scandal-Scarred SANDAG Still Can't Be Trusted. *The San Diego Union-Tribune.*

Editorial Board. (2022, December 11). Adrift SANDAG Board Needs a Reckoning. *The San Diego Union-Tribune.*

Editorial Board, (2023, March 31). Fletcher's Stunning Abuse of Power. *The San Diego Union-Tribune.*

Editorial Board. (2023, August 6). Ikhrata Doomed By His Disdain For Politics. *The San Diego Union-Tribune.*

Editorial Board. (2024, April 5). Fed's Probe of SANDAG A Welcome Development. *The San Diego Union-Tribune.*

Editorial Board. (2024, October 6). Reject Measure G: SANDAG is Dishonest, Dysfunctional. *The San Diego Union-Tribune.*

Edmond, A. C. (2011). Strategies for Learning From Failure. *Harvard Business Review, 89*(4).

Erie, S., Kogan, V., & Mackenzie, S.A. (2011). *Paradise Plundered: Fiscal Crisis and Governance Failures in San Diego.* Stanford, CA: Stanford University Press.

Fien, G. (2022, November-December). Revitalizing Culture in the World of Hybrid Work. *Harvard Business Review, 100(6)*, 17-21.

Garrick, D. (2016, March 11). Filner Harassment Civil Trial To Begin Today. *The San Diego Union-Tribune.*

Glaser, B. & Strauss, A. 1967. *The Discovery of Grounded Theory: Strategies for Qualitative Research.* New York, NY: Aldine Publishing Company.

Gottfriend, S. (2019, September 25). The Science Behind Why People Gossip—and When It Can Be a Good Thing. *Time, Inc.*

Greaves, J., & Watkins, E. (2021). *Team Emotional Intelligence 2.0.* San Diego, CA: TalentSmart.

Groupthink, Revised Edition [Film]. (1998) CRM Films.

Haines, S. (2000) *The Systems Thinking Approach to Strategic Planning and Management.* Boca Raton, FL: CRC Press.

Halverstadt, L., Elmer, M., & Wood, M. (2022, April 27). Morning Report: Ex-City Real Estate Chief Unloads Under Oath on 101 Ash. *Voice of San Diego.*

Halverstadt, L., Lopez-Villafaña, A., Elmer, M., & Keatts, A. (2023, April 21). Morning Report: With Fletcher Gone, MTS Fails to Select New Leader. *Voice of San Diego.*

Hargrove, D., Hansen, B, & Jones, T. (2019, March 19). "San Diego Water Department Insider Blames Billing Complaints on Mismanagement," *NBC San Diego.*

Ho, P. (2012, October 1). Coping with Complexity. *McKinsey & Company.*

Jennewein, C. and Stone, K. (2023, March 30). Fletcher Resignation Effective May 15, Supervisors Can Appoint a Successor or Call a Special Election. *Times of San Diego.*

Jones, H. (2020, January 8). The Rope Behind Poway's Water Problems Had Been There A Long Time. *The San Diego Union-Tribune.*

Jones, T. & Consumer, B. (2019, February 8). City Admits Water Billing Mistake, Hundreds of Customers Overcharged. *NBC San Diego.*

Kahneman, D. (2011). *Thinking, Fast and Slow.* New York, NY: Farrar, Straus, and Giroux.

Keatts, A. (2017, July 11). SANDAG Misled Voters on 2004 Tax Measure, Showing Pattern of Deception Goes Back at Least 13 Years. *Voice of San Diego.*

Keatts, A. (2020, May 20). SDPD Has the Most Untested Rape Kits in the State-by Far." *Voice of San Diego.*

Keatts, A. (2023, April 3). MTS Said It Was Investigating the Fletcher Scandal. It Isn't. *Voice of San Diego.*

Knickmeyer, E. & Smith, S. (2016, March 10). Huge water district hit with a rare federal fine. *The San Diego Union-Tribune.*

Koran, M. (2016, February 2). What Brought Marne Foster Down. *Voice of San Diego.*

Krippendorf, K. (2018). *Content Analysis: An Introduction for its Methodology* (Fourth Edition). Thousand Oaks, CA: Sage Publications.

Kuehne, M. (2021, June 1). Focus on Good Government is Critical As Cities Navigate Challenging Times. *Western City Magazine.*

Lencioni, P. (2002). *The Five Dysfunctions of Teams.* San Francisco, CA: Jossey-Bass.

Lenney. J., Lutz, B, Schüle, F., & Sheiner, L. (2021, March 24). The Sustainability of State and Local Government Pensions: A Public Finance Approach. *Brookings Papers on Economic Activity.*

Libby, S. (2017, February 20). A Reader's Guide to the SANDAG Scandal. *Voice of San Diego.*

McDonald, J. (2016, March 4). Whistleblower CFO Says Taxpayers Were Billed Before Outlays. *The San Diego Union-Tribune.*

McDonald, J. (2020, April 25). City Council to Consider Ash Street Litigation in a Third Closed Session. *The San Diego Union-Tribune.*

McDonald, J. (2021, May 9). Former Cal State San Marcos Dean Now Under Criminal Investigation. *The San Diego Union-Tribune.*

McDonald, J. (2021, July 5). Anatomy of the Deal: What Happened on Ash Street. *The San Diego Union-Tribune.*

McDonald, J. (2022, July 26). City Council Approves Controversial Ash Street Settlement Deal. *The San Diego Union-Tribune.*

McDonald, J. (2023, December 3). Broken Tolling Software, Lax Oversight: A New Lawsuit Against SANDAG Echoes Audit's Critique of Its Practices. *The San Diego Union-Tribune.*

McDonald, J. (2024, March 30). SANDAG Facing Probe by Federal Agents. *The San Diego Union-Tribune.*

Monat, J. P. & Gannon, T. F. (2015). What is Systems Thinking? A Review of Selected Literature Plus Recommendations. *American Journal of Systems Science, 4*(1), 11-26.

Moran, G. (2014, June 20). Rec Letter Rules Don't Apply to Dumanis. *The San Diego Union-Tribune.*

Murga, T. & McDonald, J. (2023, November 6). Chula Vista Politics Roiled by Charges. *The San Diego Union-Tribune.*

Murphy, J., Rhodes, M. L., Meek, J. W., & Denyer, D. (2016). Managing the Entanglement: Complexity Leadership in Public Sector Systems. *Public Administration Review, 77*(5), 692-704

Neeley, T. & Leonard, P. (2022, May-June). Developing a Digital Mindset. *Harvard Business Review, 100*(3), 50-55.

Noonan, W. (2007). *Discussing the Undiscussable: A Guide to Overcoming Defensive Routines in the Workplace.* New Jersey: Jossey-Bass.

O'Neill, B. (2013). Leadership and the Profession: Where to From Here? *Public Management, 95*(2): 19-23.

Patterson, K., Grenny, J., & McMillan, R. (2002). *Crucial Conversations: Tools for Talking When Stakes Are High.* New York: McGraw-Hill.

Paul, M. (1997, February). Moving From Blame to Accountability. *The Systems Thinker, 8*(1), 1-6.

Place, L. (2022, October 26). Vista City Manager Resigns After Council Hampers Hiring Authority. *The Coast News.*

Reyes-Velarde, A. (2019, March 14). Instagram-Hungry Crowds are Destroying the Super Bloom. *Los Angeles Times.*

Rivard, R. (2019, April 22). Madaffer Says He's the New Sheriff in the San Diego Water World. *Voice of San Diego.*

Rocha, V. (2016, October 11). Former Port of LA Police Chief Sentenced to 2 Years in Federal Prison for Tax Evasion. *Los Angeles Times.*

Schmates, M. (2019, July 20). A Surprising New Workplace Study Reveals Who the Real Gossipers Are. *Inc.*

Schwartz, M. (2019, March 19). Poppy Apocalypse: A California City Swarmed by Selfie Stick-Toting Tourists. *NPR's All Things Considered.*

Semuels, A. (2019, November 11). A Beta Test for Big Tech's Clout. *Time.*

Senge, P. (1990). *The Fifth Discipline: The Art and Practice of Learning Organizations.* New York, NY: Currency Doubleday.

Senge, P. (1994). *The Fifth Discipline Field Book Strategies and Tools for Building a Learning Organization.* New York, NY: Currency Doubleday.

Senturia, N. (2016, October 31). White-Collar Criminals Just Assume They Won't Get Caught. *The San Diego Union-Tribune.*

Shalby, C., Lopez, R. J., & Watanabe, T. (2022, February 17). CSU Chancellor Joseph Castro Resigns Amid Scrutiny Over Handling of Sexual Misconduct Case. *Los Angeles Times.*

Sklar, D. L. (2023, April 4). Supervisors to Discuss Options for Replacing Fletcher at May 2 Meeting. *Times of San Diego.*

Smith, D. (2024, January 9). DWP Board President is Out Amid Ethics Questions, Power Struggle at Utility. *Los Angeles Times.*

Smith, D. (2024, April 24). New Head of L.A. DWP Will Make $750,000 a year—Nearly Twice As Much As Her Predecessor. *Los Angeles Times.*

Smith, E. (2024, January 14). Why LAPD Chief Michel Moore Had To Go. *Los Angeles Times*.

Smith, J. E. (2017, August 1). Investigation: SANDAG Bungled Billions in Revenue Projections and Deleted Emails Ahead of Public Vote on Transportation Tax Measure. *The San Diego Union-Tribune*.

Smith, J. E. (2022, November 22). Will San Diego's $160 Billion Rail Expansion Survive GOP Election Shake-Up? *The San Diego Union-Tribune*.

Soltes, E. (2016). *Why They Do It: Inside the Mind of the White Collar Criminal*. New York, NY: Public Affairs Publisher.

Steele, J. (2016, March 8). Admiral Caught with Porn: Didn't Know It Was This Much. *The San Diego Union-Tribune*.

Stowe, K. (2023, March 29). Supervisor Fletcher Quitting State Senate Bid to Recover from PTSD, Early Trauma. *Times of San Diego*.

The U.S. Department of Justice Opened Civil Investigation into Sexual Harassment Claims Against Andrew Cuomo. (2021, December 3). *CBS News*.

Tiernan, C. (2023, August 3). Investigation Says Top City Administrator Violated Sexual Harassment Rules; Perkins Says Mayor Okayed Him Dating Staff. *The Spokesman-Review*.

Trevino, L., and Nelson, K. (2017). *Managing Business Ethics: Straight Talk About How to Do It Right* (7th Edition). Hoboken, NJ: John Wiley and Sons.

Using Framing to Face a Challenge. (2005). *Leader to Leader, 2005*(38), 59-60.

Van Grove, J. (2023, July 13). San Diego Port CEO Joe Stuyvesant Paced On Administrative Leave. *The San Diego Union-Tribune*.

Walker, M. (2024, April 17). Boeing Whistle Blower Details His Concerns to Congressional Panel. *The New York Times*.

Walter, D. (2020, August 10). California's Immense Pension Dilemma. *CalMatters*.

Wang, Y. (2016, February 25). Ex-California State Senator Leland Yee, Gun Control Champion, Heading to Prison for Weapons Trafficking. *The Washington Post*.

Weisberg, L. (2023, July 28). SANDAG's Embattled Hasan Ikhrata to Leave Agency by End of Year. *The San Diego Union-Tribune*.

Weisberg, L. (2023, November 9). San Diego's Real Estate Director Out As City Executives Announce Department Consolidation. *The San Diego Union-Tribune*.

Yadavall, A. (2019, March 20). How Cities Around the Country Address Rising Pension Liability. *National League of Cities*.

Appendix A:

Partial List of Author's Public Sector Client Organizations, 1993–2021*

Board Governance/Board Facilitation:
CalTRUST Board of Trustees
Centre City Development Corporation Board of Directors
City of Carlsbad City Council
City of Carson, City Council
City of Escondido, City Council
City of Napa City Council
City of Newport Beach Boards and Commissions
City of San Diego Balboa Park Committee Board
City of San Diego Balboa Park Conservancy Board
City of San Diego Park and Recreation Committee/Board
City of San Juan Capistrano City Council
City of San Luis Obispo City Council
City of San Marcos City Council
Helix Water District Board of Directors
Joint Powers Insurance Agency for Water Agencies, Board of Directors
National Conference for Community and Justice Board of Directors
Otay Water District Board of Directors
Palomar Health Board of Directors
Rainbow Water District Board of Directors
Rest Haven Board of Directors
Rincon Water District Board of Directors
San Diego Association of Governments (SANDAG) Board of Directors
San Diego Convention Center Board
San Diego County Airport Authority Board of Directors

San Diego County Water Authority Board of Directors
San Diego Housing Commissioners
San Diego Unified Port District, Port Commission Board
San Miguel Fire Protection Agency Board of Directors
State of California Department of Consumer Affairs/Bureaus/Boards
Union of Pan-Asian Americans Board of Directors
YMCA Rancho Penasquitos Board of Directors

Executive Coaching, Management Consulting, OD, Workshop Facilitation, Leadership Development and Training, and/ Organizational Assessment:
Cal State University, San Bernardino
Cal State University, San Diego (SDSU)
Cal State University, San Marcos
California Association of Public Retirement Systems (CALAPRS)
California Bureau of Forensic Services
California Department of Fish and Game
California State Contractor's License Board
California State Department of Consumer Affairs
CalSTRS
CalSTRS Retirement System
Centre City Development Corporation
Chamber of Commerce, San Diego
City of Berkeley
City of Brentwood
City of Carlsbad
City of Carson
City of Chula Vista
City of Culver City
City of Encinitas
City of Escondido
City of La Mesa
City of Lake Elsinore
City of Napa
City of Newport Beach
City of Oceanside

City of Pomona
City of Porterville
City of Poway
City of Rancho Cucamonga
City of Sacramento
City of San Diego
City of San Diego Council Member Christine Kehoe's Office
City of San Diego Council Member Scott Harvey's Office
City of San Diego Council Member Toni Atkins's Office
City of San Diego Mayor's Office, Mayor Faulconer
City of San Diego Mayor's Office, Mayor Gloria
City of San Diego Mayor's Office, Mayor Golding
City of San Diego Mayor's Office, Mayor Sanders
City of San Diego Mayor's' Office, Mayor Murphy
City of San Marcos
City of Temecula
City of Visalia
City of Vista
City/County of San Francisco
County Counsel, San Diego County
County of Napa
County of San Diego Alternate Public Defenders Office
County of San Diego Public Defenders Office
County of San Diego Public Works Department
County of San Diego Treasurer/Tax Collector
Crawford High Complex
CUSH Automotive; private sector
Dupont (in partnership with TalentSmart); private sector
Helix Water District
Kearny High Complex
Los Angeles County Employees Retirement Association (LACERA)
Metropolitan Transit Authority, Los Angeles
Otay Water District
Padre Dam Water District
Pitzer College Faculty
Port of Los Angeles

Riverside Community College District
San Bernardino District Attorney's Office
San Diego Association of Governments (SANDAG)
San Diego City Employees Retirement System (SDCERS)
San Diego County Employees Retirement Association (SDCERA)
San Diego County Health and Human Services Agency
San Diego County Taxpayers Association
San Diego District Attorney's Office
San Diego Housing Commission
State Attorneys General's Office
State of California Assembly Member Christine Kehoe's Office
State of California Assembly Speaker Toni Atkins's Office;
State Senator and President Pro Tempore of the Senate Toni Atkins's Office
UCLA, Anderson School
UCSD Medical Center at Hillcrest and Thornton Hospitals
UCSD Medical Center, CEO's Office
UCSD Moore's Cancer Center, Radiation Oncology
University of San Diego, President's Office
YMCA , Rancho Penasquitos

*Dr. Sopp worked with each of these organizations, providing management consulting, board/workshop facilitation, coaching, management academies and trainings, and organization development services under the umbrella of The CENTRE/Centre for Organization Effectiveness (1993-2021).

Appendix B:

Chronological List of Select Reference Materials

In this appendix, are articles and case studies I have flagged over the years and represent public sector missteps, misjudgments and scandals. Some are referred to in the manuscript and some are not. They are offered here in chronological order (older articles to more recent articles) for the reader to peruse as desired.

Paradise Plundered: Fiscal Crisis and Governance Failures in San Diego, Stanford University Press, 2011. See Part II, Chapters 3 and 4, 61–140. Authors: Steven P. Erie, Vladimir Kogan, and Scott A. Mackenzie.

- While there were numerous articles in local and national newspapers about the pension underfunding at the City of San Diego, the book by this research team at the University of California, San Diego, and the University of California, Davis, provides the most comprehensive analysis.

"Rec Letter Rules Don't Apply to Dumanis," *The San Diego Union-Tribune,* Watchdog report, June 20, 2014. Author: Greg Moran.

- This watchdog article about a former district attorney, County of San Diego, details the internal legal special Policy Directive 33, signed by the district attorney herself, that indicates letterhead is to be used "only for the official business and work of this office." Her spokesperson indicated the policy is "intended to prevent employees from using Dumanis's name and title to imply support for a particular cause or person, and does not necessarily apply to her."

"What Brought Marne Foster Down," *Voice of San Diego* online, February 2, 2016. Author: Mario Koran.

- See this article for a full explanation of the misdeeds of a school board chair.

"Ex-California State Senator Leland Yee, Gun Control Champion, Heading to Prison for Weapons Trafficking," *The Washington Post*, February 25, 2016. Author: Yanan Wang.

- Leland Yee, a California State Senator, was caught up in an arms deal and pay-to-play scheme.

"Whistle Blower CFO Says Taxpayers Were Billed Before Outlays," *The San Diego Union-Tribune*, March 4, 2016. Author: Jeff McDonald.

- This article refers to the executive director of the Mental Health Systems Charity, who improperly billed her husband's company for expenses that did not occur, and the payment went into their personal account.

"Admiral Caught With Porn: 'Didn't Know It Was This Much,'" *The San Diego Union-Tribune*, March 8, 2016. Author: Jeanette Steele.

"Huge Water District Hit with Rare Federal Fine," *The San Diego Union-Tribune*, March 10, 2016. Associated Press.

- This story refers to comments made by Central California Wetlands Water District General Manager Thomas Birmingham that he had done "a little Enron accounting" while explaining how he arrived at the bond measure amount.

"Filner Harassment Civil Trial to Begin Today," *The San Diego Union-Tribune*, March 11, 2016. Author: David Garric.

"Former Port of LA Police Chief Sentenced to 2 Years in Federal Prison for Tax Evasion," *Los Angeles Times,* October 11, 2016. Author: Veronica Rocha.

- This story was a gut punch to the Port of Los Angeles organization as the Port of LA's Police Chief, Ronald Boyd, was competent, articulate, well-liked, and affable. As it turns out, he had a side business in security called Port Watch that had a contract with the Port of LA, something he never disclosed. He participated in the interview panel that approved awarding this contract to his very own business. His other offense was tax evasion, and this landed him in prison for two years. The biggest downfall, however, was the deception of the organization and all those who admired him.

"A Reader's Guide to the SANDAG Scandal," *Voice of San Diego* online, February 20, 2017. Author: Sara Libby.

"SANDAG Misled Voters on 2004 Tax Measure, Showing Pattern of Deception Goes Back at Least 13 Years," *Voice of San Diego* online, July 11, 2017. Author: Andrew Keatts.

"Report on Independent Examination of SANDAG Measure A Revenue Estimate Communications," July 31, 2017. Author: John C. Huesto.

"Investigation: SANDAG Bungled Billions in Revenue Projections and Deleted Emails Ahead of Public Vote on Transportation Tax Measure," *The San Diego Union-Tribune,* August 1, 2017. Editorial Board.

"SANDAG Executive Gary Gallegos to Retire Amid Scandal," *KPBS News Notes* online, August 8, 2017. Author: Andrew Bowen.

"Revamped SANDAG Won't Rebuild Trust Quickly After Its Credibility Crumbled," *The San Diego Union-Tribune,* October 13, 2017. Editorial Board.

"City Admits Water Billing Mistake, Hundreds of Customers Overcharged," *NBC Channel 7* online, February 8, 2019, updated February 9, 2019. Authors: Tom Jones and Bob Consumer.

"Instagram-Hungry Crowds are Destroying the Super Bloom," *Los Angeles Times,* March 14, 2019. Author: Alejandro Reyes Velarde.

Los Angeles Times. "Super bloom shutdown: Lake Elsinore shuts access after crowds descend on poppy fields." March 17, 2019. Author: Jaclyn Cosgrove.

"San Diego Water Department Insider Blames Billing Complaints on Mismanagement," *NBC Channel 7* online, March 19, 2019, updated March 20, 2019. Authors: Dorian Hargrove, Bob Hanse, and Tom Jones.

- Like all missteps, actions were taken once the misstep was identified. In this case, the actions taken by key players and their reactions to the critique were where the problematic behaviors occurred.

"Poppy Apocalypse: A California City Swarmed by Selfie Stick-Toting Tourists," *NPR's All Things Considered* radio show, March 19, 2019. Author: M. Schwartz.

"Madaffer Says He's the New Sheriff in the San Diego Water World," *Voice of San Diego* online, April 22, 2019. Author: Ry Rivard.

"The Rope Behind Poway's Water Problems Had Been There A Long Time," *The San Diego Union-Tribune*, January 8, 2020. Author: Harry Jones.

"City Council to Consider Ash Street Litigation in a Third Closed Session," *The San Diego Union-Tribune*, April 25, 2020. Author: Jeff McDonald.

"SDPD Has the Most Untested Rape Kits in the State—by Far," *Voice of San Diego* online, May 20, 2020. Author: Andrew Keatts.

- Again, the reaction to the critique is where the problematic behaviors occurred.

Jeff McDonald, "Former Cal State San Marcos Dean Now Under Criminal Investigation," *The San Diego Union-Tribune*, May 9, 2021. Author: Jeff McDonald.

- *The San Diego Union-Tribune* published this article about Michael Schroder, the former dean of extended studies at Cal State San

Marcos, who racked up tens of thousands of dollars in improper travel billings and was under criminal investigation. This scandal also tainted the tenure of the university's president, Karen Hughes, upon the time of her retirement.

"Anatomy of the Deal: What Happened on Ash Street," *The San Diego Union-Tribune* online, July 5, 2021. Author: Jeff McDonald.

"Andrew Cuomo Sexual Harassment: The Key Testimony From the Report," *The Guardian*, August 3, 2021. Author: Lauren Artani.

- See full investigation results for the entire context and findings: State of New York, Office of the Attorney General, "Report of Investigations of Sexual Harassment by Governor Andrew M. Cuomo," August 3, 2021

"U.S. Department of Justice Opened Civil Investigation into Sexual Harassment Claims Against Andrew Cuomo," December 3, 2021. CBS News online, AP.

Shalby, C., et al. "CSU Chancellor Joseph Castro Resigns Amid Scrutiny Over Handling of Sexual Misconduct Case," *Los Angeles Times* online, February 17, 2022.

"Blithe Spending of Public Funds Shows Scandal-Scarred SANDAG Still Can't Be Trusted," *The San Diego Union-Tribune*, April 16, 2022. Editorial Board.

- Further evidence of the impact of previous SANDAG missteps is that the "blithe" spending referred to in this article turned out not to be reckless at all; upon further inspection by internal staff, nearly all expenses were within proper guidelines, but the press was quick to critique and accept initial audit conclusions without further review because the organization was on the radar.

"Morning Report: Ex-City Real Estate Chief Unloads Under Oath on 101 Ash," *Voice of San Diego* online, April 27, 2022. Author: Scott Lewis.

"City Council Approves Controversial Ash Street Settlement Deal," *The San Diego Union-Tribune*, July 26, 2022. Author: Jeff McDonald.

Archie, "Andrew Cuomo files a complaint against Letitia James for her sexual harassment report," *NPR* online, September 14, 2022. Author: A. Archie.

- It should be noted that as of this book's writing, Cuomo was suing the New York State Attorney General on the charges brought forth to clear his name.

"Former Cal State chancellor displayed "blind spot" to complaints of sexual harassment at Fresno State," *EdSource*, September 29, 2022. Author: A. Smith.

"Vista City Manager Resigns After Council Hampers Hiring Authority," *The Coast News*, October 26, 2022. Author: Laura Place.

"Will San Diego's $160 Billion Rail Expansion Survive GOP Election Shake Up?" *The San Diego Union-Tribune*, November 22, 2022. Author: Joshua Emerson Smith.

"Adrift SANDAG Board Needs a Reckoning," *The San Diego Union-Tribune,* December 11, 2022. Editorial.

"SANDAG's Divided Board Off to a Rocky Year After Small City Walkout," *Voice of San Diego* online, January 19, 2023. Author: Jennifer Bowman.

"What is Next for City's Ash Street Boondoggle," *The San Diego Union-Tribune,* March 26, 2023. Author: Jeff McDonald.

"Supervisor Fletcher Quitting State Senate Bid to Recover from PTSD, Early Trauma," *Times of San Diego* online, March 29, 2023. Author: Ken Stowe.

"Fletcher Resignation Effective May 15, Supervisors Can Appoint Successor or Call Special Election," *Times of San Diego* online, March 30, 2023. Authors: Chris Jennewein and Ken Stowe.

"Fletcher's Stunning Abuse of Power." *The San Diego Union-Tribune,* March 31, 2023. Editorial Board.

"MTS Said It Was Investigating the Fletcher Scandal. It Isn't,*" Voice of San Diego* online, April 3, 2023. Author: Andrew Keatts.

"Supervisors to Discuss Options for Replacing Fletcher at May 2 Meeting," *Times of San Diego* online, April 4, 2023. Author: Debbie L. Sklar.

"Fletcher Controversy is One In a Long Line of Democrat Sex Scandals," KPBS Midday Edition online, April 11, 2023. Authors: M. Cavanaugh, et. al.

"With Fletcher Gone, MTS Fails to Select New Leader," *Voice of San Diego Morning Report* online, April 21, 2023.Authors: Lisa Halverson, et.al.

"San Diego Port CEO Joe Stuyvesant Paced On Administrative Leave," *The San Diego Union-Tribune,* July 13, 2023. Author: J. Van Grove.

"Ex-USC Dean Sentenced to Home Confinement," *Los Angeles Times,* July 25, 2023. Associated Press.

"SANDAG's Embattled Hasan Ikhrata to Leave Agency by End of Year," *The San Diego Union-Tribune,* July 28, 2023.Author: L. Weisberg.

"Investigation Says Top City Administrator Violated Sexual Harassment Rules; Perkins Says Mayor Okayed Him Dating Staff," The Spokesman-Review, online, August 3, 2023. Author: C. Tiernan.

"Ikhrata Doomed By His Disdain For Politics," *The San Diego Union-Tribune,* August 6, 2023. Editorial Board.

"Chula Vista Politics Roiled by Charges," *The San Diego Union-Tribune,* November 6, 2023. Authors: T. Murga and J. McDonald.

"Broken Tolling Software, Lax Oversight: A New Lawsuit Against SANDAG Echoes Audit's Critique of Its Practices," *The San Diego Union-Tribune* online, December 3, 2023. Author: J. McDonald.

"Metropolitan Water District of So. Cal: Leadership's Fallen and It Can't Get Up," *MWD Water Watch,* January 4, 2024. Author: T. Butka.

"DWP Board President is Out Amid Ethics Questions, Power Struggle at Utility," *LA Times.com*, January 9, 2024. Author: D. Smith.

"Why LAPD Chief Michel Moore Had To Go," *Los Angeles Times*, January 14, 2024. Author: E. Smith.

"SANDAG Facing Probe by Federal Agents," *The San Diego Union-Tribune*, March 30, 2024. Author: Jeff McDonald.

"Fed's Probe of SANDAG A Welcome Development," *The San Diego Union-Tribune*, April 5, 2024. Editorial Board.

"Boeing Whistle Blower Details His Concerns to Congressional Panel," *The New York Times*, April 17, 2024. Author: Mark Walker.

"New Head of L.A. DWP Will Make $750,000 a year—Nearly Twice As Much As Her Predecessor," *LA Times.com,* April 24, 2024. Author: A. Smith.

"Oakland Mayor in Crisis As Lawyer, Top Aide Jump Ship Following Fiery Speech after FBI Raid," *LA Times.com*, June 25, 2024. Author: N. Goldberg.

"Reject Measure G: SANDAG is Dishonest, Dysfunctional," The San Diego Union-Tribune online, October 6, 2024. Editorial Board.

Acknowledgments

The League of California Cities "2020 Annual Conference for City Managers" deserves credit for jump-staring this manuscript. The program committee invited me to be the concluding conference keynote speaker and share the themes covered in these chapters. Given the topic, this request held some risk for them. My preparation for the keynote became the blueprint for this manuscript. An acknowledgement to **Scott Chadwick** for the role he played in the conference invite and a special "thank you" to **Danell Scarborough, Ed.D**, a skilled colleague in the field of change and respectful work environments, who sent a timely text to me minutes before that speech. Realizing I was facing a potentially resistant audience, she reminded me that I was known for "truth telling and straight talk" and not to waiver.

Jean Greaves, Ph.D., a published author in the field of emotional intelligence, offered to review an early draft of the first few chapters and provided a tutorial about editing, publishing, and book titles. I am grateful she has has hung in there with me the entire time as an experienced resource for absolutely everything.

As I became concerned that early drafts might read like a "tell all," I turned to a respected and retired city attorney, **Celia Brewer**, whose judgment I trusted. She read my draft, immediately saw my dilemma, and encouraged me to use pseudonyms for the players and neutral terms for agencies/cities/counties in order not to distract the reader. Her insistence was that this would turn the reader's attention to the learnings in the examples instead of to the players. She was spot on.

My sincere appreciation to the many respected top-level public sector leaders who I asked to weigh-in on my drafts along the way. **Jaymie Bradford** read an early draft, supported and appreciated the findings, and reminds me every time I see her how it has stayed with her. **Sandy Kerl** gave a thumbs up and provided an important nudge for me to dig deeper when describing the difficult decisions about how and when to step down. **Danell** continued to be an important cheerleader throughout the writing process as did the zoom group of **OEPer's Daryl Grisby, Tom Packard,** the late **Robin Reid,** and **Richel Thaler. Richel** in particular provided critical support when she indicated my findings and conclusions were applicable in her world of public universities. **Patricia Frazier** and **Denice Garcia** were steadfast, loyal, and interested supporters.

An unexpected source of support came during a small gathering at the home of **Toni G. Atkins**, while she was Senator and President Pro tempore of the California State Senate. She surprised me by asking that I discuss my manuscript. The smart and accomplished women in her living room immediately jumped in to provide advice on publication and public relations strategies. Throughout, **Drs. Joyce and Rick Ross** always let me know they were in my corner and Joyce especially felt the book would be an important contribution to the field of public administration.

For me, the stars of this book are the top-level public sector leaders I interviewed to understand their perspective about why and how their careers had ended so well. These are top-level public sector leaders I had consulted with and facilitated workshops for over the course of my career and watched them practice their craft. I came back to them years later as I had identified my own notion of what worked, what it takes to avoid a misstep, misjudgment, or scandal. I wanted to hear their thinking. I offer my deep gratitude for their time and willingness to share their reflections over coffee and lunches over many, many years. A heartfelt thank you to: **Frank Belock; Kevin Crawford; the late Walt Ekard; Stacey LoMedico; Dana Smith; Stacey Stevenson; Mark Weston; and Grant Yates.**

A special nod to **Craig Dunn, Ph.D.,** Professor Emeritus, Western Washington University. His thorough knowledge of philosophy and ethical management principles will stay with me forever.

An acknowledgement to the public libraries across California where I did a lot of my writing and who always provide a scholarly environment to work in. In particular, Pacific Grove Public Library, San Diego's Northern Community Public Library, UCSD Geisel Library, and our own book-filled garage office library. Hector Rodriguez, project director with Panda Publishing Agency, has been constant in his patience and support. No change or correction was too minor for Hector and his team to respond to and I am grateful for the significant role they played in getting this manuscript to publication.

My final appreciation is to **my family**: daughters Kyla Thomas, Ph.D., and Kaitlin Thomas, Ph.D., their supportive spouses, Ping and Jean-Eric, their smart and engaging children, and the "Poppy" of our family, Hayden Thomas, Ph.D., my partner and husband since 1972. Kyla scoured the notes, bibliography, chapter titles, and manuscript content to fine-tune it and clean up any confusing verbiage. She pushed back on my thinking in important ways. Kaitlin helped with formatting graphs, technical issues that perplexed me, thoroughly researched and documented publishing options and angles on book titles, and calmly and reassuringly safeguarded my work. Both daughters looked out for me during this process. I thank their spouses for taking over the grandies while their moms were helping me. I thank our grandies, for giving me a true break anytime I would take care of them. They filled my heart and gave me a time-out from administrative worries and the intensity of writing.

There are no words to adequately express my gratitude and appreciation to Hayden. He was my greatest cheerleader and toughest critic especially when he saw me start to soften and back away from my style of writing. He read every single draft. He is a critical theorist and insists on clarity. He has always made me a better person, professional, and writer. He has never let me down except about handling certain home errands and to do's in a timely manner.

My mother, Angela Sopp, passed away during the earliest stages of my writing this book. If she were still living, she would, of course, take complete credit for this accomplishment.

Author Biography

Trudy Sopp has spent a rewarding professional career in the complex and demanding public sector. She managed the City of San Diego's organization effectiveness unit which received award-winning recognition for its change efforts, and founded The Centre for Organization Effectiveness, a California Joint Powers Authority. Established in 1993, The Centre provides leadership development academies and forums, organization development interventions, consulting, and coaching to public, non-profit, and private organizations.

Since founding The Centre, Trudy has been a frequent keynote speaker and consultant to state and local elected officials, city managers, county administrators, boards and commissions, water agencies, educational and healthcare institutions, non-profit agencies, and private sector companies.

Trudy holds a Ph.D. ('82) in Sociology in Education, University of Toronto, Ontario Institute for Studies in Education and, since 2014, has been a lecturer in ethical decision-making at the Fowler College of Business, San Diego State University. She and her husband, Hayden, have two brilliant daughters, two perfect sons-in-law, and three delightful grandies.

www.ingramcontent.com/pod-product-compliance
Lightning Source LLC
Chambersburg PA
CBHW051246020426
42333CB00025B/3074